Abhaynath Mishra, PhD has sought and found a most relatable metaphor for matters that matter — the quest for inner equilibrium, the search for balance in external forces, and the ideal of bringing the two within a symbiotic whole - all in the way Narmada reveals itself to us. It is a must read: the metaphor recommends itself.

Narendra Jha, *Journalist*

Reading gives a feeling of actually being on the Narmada Parikrama traversing over satiating material creation to a blissful world....

Shankar Thakur, *Geo Scientist, ONGC*

The book is a pointer to a rich culture, Divine consciousness and the way Narmada Mai looks after her sincere devotees. A must read to understand spirituality in its true sense.

Shravan Chemburkar,
ex- Chief Operating Officer, Bombay Gymkhana

'Dawn of Reality' is a profound book most needed in today's trying times. Vivid description of his 'Parikrama', interactions with the Sages and the satsangs are mind blowing.

Saraswathi Mahadevan, *Entrepreneur*

The Author has beautifully described continuum of the journey from 'I and Mine' leading to distress; to 'Universal Consciousness' the arena of ultimate bliss....

Prasenjit Pukhan, *Vice President – People and Culture*

The narrations on life, personality and spirituality are enriching and profound. Approach in addressing life's questions, offering apt analogies, and resolving uncertainties is truly remarkable.

Hare Krishna, *Spiritual Enquirer*

Synthesis of path to wisdom, selfless action and exclusive devotion is the highlight of the book.

Sachin Jha, *National Sales Manager, Neonatal*

Dawn of Reality
Unfolding Life's Hidden Treasures

Abhaynath Mishra, PhD

BLACK EAGLE BOOKS
Dublin, USA | Bhubaneswar, India

 Black Eagle Books
USA address:
7464 Wisdom Lane
Dublin, OH 43016

India address:
E/312, Trident Galaxy, Kalinga Nagar,
Bhubaneswar-751003, Odisha, India

E-mail: info@blackeaglebooks.org
Website: www.blackeaglebooks.org

First International Edition Published by
Black Eagle Books, 2023

DAWN OF REALITY
Unfolding Life's Hidden Treasures
by **Abhaynath Mishra, PhD**

Copyright © Abhaynath Mishra, PhD

All rights reserved. No part of this publication may be reproduced, stored in a retrieval system, or transmitted, in any form or by any means, electronic, mechanical, photocopying, recording or otherwise without the prior permission of the publisher.

Cover: **Ms. Meenakshi Mishra**

Interior Design: Ezy's Publication

ISBN- 978-1-64560-428-0 (Paperback)
Library of Congress Control Number: 2023943796

Printed in the United States of America

Dedicated to
Narmada Mai

Inspiration to make this cover:

Harmonious development of head, heart and senses is the surest means of growing into the highest goal of life. The OM represents the realisation of the infinite potential. The waves of the Narmada River inspire faith, love, compassion and devotion. Dawn marks the beginning of twilight before the sun rises and life begins. As the sun slowly rises above the horizon, it brings a burst of vibrant colours that fill the sky with energy and life to awaken and illuminate humanity. No matter how dark our nights may be, the sunrise reminds us that hope is always on the horizon.

Narmada Udgam Sthan, Amarkantak, Madhya Pradesh

Justice Harish Chandra Mishra

HIGH COURT OF JHARKHAND
RANCHI - 834 033

Ranchi, the 15th of March, 2021

MESSAGE

I consider myself a blessed self, for getting the opportunity of going through the soft copy of the book **"Dawn of Reality"** authored by Mr. Abhaynath Mishra (Ph.D.).

The initial cursory and casual look to the book soon transformed into an interesting reading. As I turned into the pages, I found myself in a different world altogether – the world of spirituality and imaginations.

Mr. Mishra is one of the most fortunate person to have undertaken the **NARMADA YATRA**, in spite of his very busy schedule in his enterprise at Mumbai. For the benefit of others, he has penned down his experiences of the YATRA in a very lucid and interesting manner. His spiritual gains during the YATRA in discourses with the enlightened Sages, during Satsang with them, and even his own experiences during the YATRA, are beyond comprehension and give a very interesting reading. Fortunate are those who get the opportunity of such Satsang. Goswami Tulsidas has very aptly said:

"तात स्वर्ग अपवर्ग सुख धरिअ तुला एक अंग
तूल न ताहि सकल मिलि जो सुख लव सत्संग।"

Fortunate shall be even those who get the opportunity to read about such discourses in this book.

The extraordinary experiences that Mr. Mishra witnessed with the blessings of Mother Narmada, whenever he was in distress during the Yatra, have only to be believed, as they are beyond any explanation and comprehension.

I am confident that this book shall be of immense benefit to the Seekers.

"Narmade Har"

15/3/2021

(Jusice H.C. Mishra)

Preface

Times have gone by with innovations, globalisation, and changes taking place at an unthinkable speed due to science and technology overtaking it all. We have forgotten our values of life and respect for the environment, which we have destroyed. Environmental pressures, societal re-organisation, social media indulgence, and involvement in worldly matters have led man to become greedy and hateful and indulge in unethical practices that have disturbed the equilibrium of a blissful life.

Lust and attachment are responsible for the universe's creation, existence, and maintenance; however, it is also the root cause of ignorance and false understanding of "I" and "Mine." Human beings spend their prime energy trying to fulfil their desires at the cost of their spiritual growth, mental peace and happiness. Ego, lust, greed, hatred, jealousy, curiosity, thoughts, ideas, and consequences behave strangely. While an individual undergoes the process of change, his perception, belief, concept and energy keep shifting, giving rise to newer thoughts, feelings, and actions. Due to a lack of self-awareness, individuals commit mistakes and defend themselves. They act with limited knowledge and gradually move down the winding lane, which leads to misery and unethical behaviour.

Everyone desires happiness; unfortunately, the majority,

including the upper-class fraternity, remains unhappy and spends crucial energy satisfying worldly longings. They are busy accumulating wealth, fame or legacy, accompanying relationships, mental, emotional, physical and social discomfort.

Engaging in ethical activities is beneficial to all. Having good personal and social conduct is most conducive to humanity. Good people are generally deprived of materialistic things but are happier than those with power and wealth! In the nineteenth verse of Bhaja Govindam, Saint Adi Shankaracharya rightly narrates that an individual may like meditative practices or worldly pleasures, may be attached or detached, still only the individual fixing his mind on the Divine lovingly enjoys lasting bliss.

Philosophy aims to transcend an individual to overcome human suffering in a well-defined manner. Walking the steps is based on an individual's capability and capacity to understand and follow the supreme knowledge of self-realisation. Spiritual knowledge is a matter beyond the range of sense apprehension. An individual has to commit to a disciplinary pursuit of scriptures or seek the right knowledge from a spiritual guru or experience it through exceptional experiences. Scriptures, Saints, Rishis, and philosophers have dwelt upon human proficiency and efficiency, and knowledge of the same is central to blissful living. Individuals must walk on the defined path proposed in the scriptures, with devotion and discipline, for their composite self-development.

Existence is complete in itself. Times, values, and situations obligate individuals to right or wrong behaviour. Aligning consciousness, will, intellect, mind, and feelings brings an awakening and a vibrant state. Ignorance arises out of Maya, which is the cause of all our miseries. Ignorance leads to jealousy, anger, and hatred, whereas love, compassion, enthusiasm and care arise from the right knowledge. In spirituality, an uninterrupted link between a devotee's spiritual attitude and the behavioural aspect of proper conduct is a must. Hearing, contemplating, living and breathing the truth are pillars of spiritual upliftment. The steadiness of mind, faith and observance of spiritual conduct come from studying scriptures, listening to discourses of realised Saints, selfless service, meditation, devotion to the Divine, and soaking the self in self-consciousness.

Many Saints and Munis hidden from the world's eye are in deep penance in remote locations on the banks of the Narmada. They are enlightened beings whose knowledge, spirituality, sacrifice, compassion, and love outshine everything. They care for their disciples and parikramawasis' spiritual needs of self-transformation and lasting happiness. Their teachings' common themes are definite and walkable steps for self-realisation and blissful living.

On attaining a certain degree of spiritual maturity, Saints undertake a long spiritual journey in isolation or remote locations for deeper experiences in pursuit of their spiritual advancement. A compelling force within had been pulling me to clear the complexity and drama of the creation and gain the supreme spiritual knowledge which leads to a happy, calm, and blissful state. I longed for an exceptional experience of circumambulation of the Narmada River, as it has enlightened numerous Saints.

Narmada Parikrama is a laboratory to experiment with - the law of spirituality, the ecstasy of nature, the company of enlightened Saints, Vedic culture, India's glory, and an appropriate path for self-transformation. Parikrama lays down a comprehensive and integrated approach to self-realisation. It is a synthesis of wisdom practices, selfless action and exclusive devotion to the Lord to awaken awareness of the Divinity within. It helps remove defects of the mind - impurity, tossing, or veil. Knowledge of the pure self is facilitated by the Divine as a seeker commits self to sewa, sadhana and meditation.

Narmada Parikrama has a pre-designed path for a parikramawasi to attain self-realisation and absolute bliss. During Narmada Parikrama, divine knowledge starts unfolding from day one, and the momentum builds through discourse, grace, immersion, mantra chanting, meditation, virtues, and new habits. Indeed, a great experience!

I learnt the importance of proper nutrition, personal observances, moral conduct, and ethical code, as growth and lasting happiness begin with purity and cleanliness of the physical, mental, and emotional being. Craving for outward desires lost significance, and I got attracted to healthy food habits, body postures, and optimal breathing. I committed myself to the Divine. In return, I gained awareness from spiritual places, exceptional help from bhakts, and blessings from Saints, gurus, pundits, human beings, nature and resilience from the environment.

The warmth shown to parikramawasis by bhakts settled along the banks of Narmada Mai was exemplary. Bhakts went out of their way to serve and help without any expectation. Their hospitality was far more compassionate than can be perceived. Bhakts taught me to live with grace, humility, compassion and sacrifice. Saints, Munis, and pundits gave me insight into the fundamental truths about the universe, awareness of the self, and life's significance.

Walking through the forest, greenery, and rocky terrain during parikrama steered me through hardships, wonder and fulfilment. It helped me eliminate self-limitations. The expanse of the landscape gave me a lot of learnings, happiness and peace.

I developed a deep bond with devotion, and it helped me subdue my ego and jealousy. I did witness my negative memories, propensities, impurities, and flaws getting dissolved. I learnt to communicate with respect and dignity and be modest with words. With love and devotion, sadachar and sadhana, my energy remained vibrant and alive, and love spread within and outside.

I got a lot of inspiration and new experiences, adding to my knowledge, love, patience, peace, and confidence. It did remove the clay and uncovered the truth within. My dreams, talents, and desires got refined while discovering and fulfilling my vision to know "Who am I." I learnt the path to self-realisation and must walk the same to find my true self.

Parikrama enhanced my endurance, and I adapted a new way of living over time. I loved it, and now I miss it. I enjoyed a certain degree of spiritual intellect. I gained a vision and comprehension of the scripture with the right attitude to understand and experience it. Spiritual practices made me happy and blissful. Now I can comprehend the clarity of steps required to achieve lasting happiness.

Practice, Practice, and Practice.
OM Peace, Peace, Peace
Narmade Har.

Acknowledgement

It is only possible to venture into Narmada Parikrama with Narmada Mai's blessings. She blessed me with the darshan of all three kinds of tirthas which helped me enhance the divine knowledge and anubhava (exceptional spiritual experiences) beyond the comprehension of my senses, mind, or intellect. This experience helped me unfold many solutions to the perennial human quest for fullness. I pray she gracefully accepts my gratitude and grants me the opportunity to unveil the profound wisdom that helps me comprehend - "Who am I."

I am indebted to my Guru, whose blessings are always with me. I was privileged to be in the company of enlightened Saints and learned bhakts. Spiritual discourses with them helped me understand, and clarify doubts about the essence of Sanatana Dharma and plunge into spiritual experiences strongly endowed with a sense of reality. I am grateful to the people from Narmada Valley and fellow parikramawasis for their love, care, and forgiveness showered on me throughout the journey. I express my appreciation and bow down to them for their blessings, love, compassion, and forgiveness.

Words are not enough to express my gratefulness towards my father, Mr Indranath Mishra, and mother, Mrs Vijay Lakshmi Mishra, for their continuous support in my entire endeavour. Of course, it caused them great anxiety, but they still supported and blessed me.

My wife Neeru and daughters Maithili and Meenakshi have supported and encouraged me throughout my journey. My wife has always encouraged and strengthened my spiritual endeavour despite the pressing demands of harmonious family life. During my extended absence on my introspective quest and spiritual journeys, she conscientiously and patiently took care of the family. I am thankful to them for all this and much more.

I am thankful to my father for his time and effort in editing the manuscript and to Mr Shravan Chemburkar and Ms Saraswathi Mahadevan for diligently proofreading the draft of this work.

OM Peace, Peace, Peace

Narmade Har.

CONTENTS

Preface	xi
Acknowledgements	xvii
Unfolding	01
Narmada	08
Foundation	18
Building Blocks	39
Immersion	62
Virtue	84
Grace	96
Knowledge	108
Alignment	124
Expansion	147
Reinforcement	157
Reality	189

Unfolding

Raja (King) Janak was in deep sleep when his sentry woke him up, saying the enemy had come to the borders and war was imminent. Janak got ready and ordered his Generals to move to the country's frontline along with adequate forces and fight until they defeated the enemy fearlessly. He led the war with his army's most advanced and equipped units. War continued for a long time, and he and his other personnel got injured during the fight. After a prolonged war, the enemy defeated Janak and his army. Janak, in a captive state, was brought to the opposition camp. The King of the enemy camp told Janak, "I am the ruler of this kingdom. I can punish you; however, I will set you free with the condition that you move out of this kingdom". Raja Janak limped and slowly exited the country's territory in mental, emotional, and physical exhaustion. As he crossed the country, he saw a long queue of people with bowls waiting for their turn for free meals. When his turn came, the food was over. The organiser told him that the starch of the rice was left. Since he was starving and tired, he took the leftover, and as he moved forward, an eagle dived down and snatched the bowl.

Raja Janak suddenly woke up in a terrifying state and saw himself on his bed in the room. He asked his staff, "Is this true?" or "Was that true?" No one was able to comprehend what Raja Janak was asking. Finally, they called their superior; however, no one could understand what he was asking, nor was there any clarity of what was happening. Janak kept repeating in a mesmerised state, "Is this true?" or "Was that true."

Advancement in lifestyle, agriculture, science, technology, arts, and commerce is excelling. The innovation ceiling is increasing, and the standard of living and comfort are becoming more than decent. However, even with material advancement, the happiness quotient in society has declined due to more than the required desire, attachment, fear, jealousy, pride, ego, stress, miseries, conflict, disease, etc. Due to a chaotic lifestyle, the essence of our life has changed. Everyone is busy chasing material aspects of life, like accumulating worldly knowledge and wealth, exotic food, expensive lifestyle, excessive attachment towards community, and societal recognition. Ultimately, an individual would have to leave behind all the worldly wealth upon death, which people do not realise.

Civilisation and culture are two distinct aspects, and history has witnessed convergence or diversion from each other. The advancement of civilisation may or may not contribute to the refinement of culture. Culture inspires a holistic approach to living morally and ethically and utilises improvements for the long-term best interest. Ramayana depicted distinct civilisations and cultures of Ayodhya, Kiskindha, and Lanka during the same period. Ayodhya represents advanced civilisation and culture. Ethics, morals, and equality were pillars of governance, focusing on selfless management and community growth. Kiskindha was a prosperous province; sensual pleasures and excessive consumption of liquor were rampant, and its leader had illicit relationships with his brother's wife. In terms of culture, it was midway between Ayodhya and Lanka. Lanka was the city of gold. Its wealth came from the booty of wars and unethical, self-centred, and ruthless practices. The King sacrificed his brothers and sons to fulfil his ego. Though wealthy, Kiskindha and Lanka had an undesired and unacceptable culture. The prime reason for existence was wealth accumulation, ego fulfilment, and sensual pleasures.

In my experience, I have seen two types of happy people – those who have nothing or enlightened individuals. By the roadside, especially under the bridges in Mumbai, I see children of beggars or roadside hawkers happily sharing their food and playing with themselves. On the other side of the spectrum, in the wealthy society, kids have everything they require - maids to take care of them, family to support, doctors to attend to the slightest cause of even a sneeze, and the best food on their plates. It is arduous to feed these kids, make them play with others or keep them unconditionally happy. On the other hand, a Saint having meagre resources provides food free of cost to all his disciples and manages a happy, calm, and blissful atmosphere around him. Unfortunately, the majority of people waste their prime energy on illusionary happiness. The goal is to satisfy lust, mundane desires, and the accumulation of trivial worldly wealth or fame.

Spiritual knowledge and exceptional experiences reveal the fundamental truth about the universe and the significance of life beyond any doubt. It offers direct insight into the nature of reality and is the ultimate source of divine knowledge. As mentioned in Puran, discourse between Sanat Kumara and Sukhdev has spelt the path of self-liberation from material existence. To move from unhappiness to a blissful state, an individual needs to unveil their true nature by acquiring knowledge through sutras (scripture), manana (rational reflection), smiriti (experience of spiritual authorities), and anubhava (special occasions). The desire to live in a community leads to bondage. Investing intelligence in worldly affairs and attachment to objects of bodily senses leads to misery, whereas renunciation brings lasting happiness. Having tolerance and forgiving others is an individual's greatest strength. Being truthful and engaging in ethical activities benefits all, and displaying good behaviour is most conducive to humanity. Individuals should restrain from ego, lust, greed, anger, hatred, and jealousy to ensure self-welfare. The highest ethical principle is to be compassionate and refrain from cruelty. Renouncing desires for material enjoyment releases the individual from a host of miseries. At the time of death, only fruits of the individual karma (pious and sinful acts) accompany the soul.

Life is a continuity of births and deaths. As such, there is a link between past, present and future. Birth is a combined effort of an individual's action (karma) and attributes of his gunas (satwa, rajas or tamas). An individual's body and senses are the utmost friends when it is under their control and the greatest enemy when the person is under their control. Environmental pressure, societal re-organisation, competitive threat, technology up-gradation, social media indulgence, aspiration, and inspiration in worldly matters create struggles, proficiency pressures, and health issues. In the age of social media with information overload, individuals' systems and senses focus outwardly, resulting in energy dissipation. People wither not because of the real cause but rather due to uncertainty arising from a false sense of fear and insecurity.

Mind, ego, curiosity, thoughts, ideas, and consequences are strange phenomena. An individual gets inspiration from within or otherwise from outside interactions for thinking or doing something, with or without instructions and directions. Everything seen or visualised consists of energy - the subtlest is the mind, and on the other side of the spectrum is the expanse of the whole universe. Individuals go to the grind to fulfilling their desires rather than needs. They move through the cycle of birth, sustenance, and destruction. As they undergo the change process, their energy, perception, belief, and concept keep shifting, giving rise to newer thoughts, feelings, and actions. To bridge the gap between micro and macro, an individual needs to drill self and social restraints within, act ethically, avoid selfish attachments and accept them without positive or negative feelings.

The world operates through a constant cycle of reciprocity. People breathe in and exhale, experience sleep and wakefullness. They exchange money for goods, offer services in return for compensation, nurture children to fulfill their bonds, and seek and offer grace and protection. Products, services, or wealth have limited tenure and diminishing return in terms of happiness. The longing for more is insatiable akin to a bottomless well. The more one possesses, the more appetite for acquisition.

In a spiritual discussion, I was asked, "In what condition will you return a borrowed item from your friend?" My natural response was - in the same condition that I had borrowed the item. The next line of discussion took a twist- "In what condition will you return yourself to Divine." It took some time to understand the statement. Finally, with help, the solution was that the Divine had sent us into this world in a blissful and happy state. Therefore, we must remain satisfied and return our life to the Divine in a pleasant and cheerful nature. Nevertheless, how?

The solution is simple - face your mind inward, stay calm and blissful in good and bad moments. In life's journey, an individual should be satisfied when the result is as per expectation and contented when it is not. Problems act as a safety valve that saves us from many unseen obstacles of severe nature. Wealth earned through unethical means brings arrogance, hostility, jealousy, disgust, and other problems. In contrast, Saints who have nothing lead a happy life.

The Divine has sent us into this world as healthy and cheerful beings. However, our thoughts and actions are responsible for diseases or obstacles. It is an opportunity to build connections and relationships with the Divine and have a meaningful relationship with our inner-self. Experience compassion and love, pay gratitude for our well-being, imbibe forgiveness, and move forward. The teaching left a deep impression and intensified my quest to look for a Spiritual Guru to pull me up to a state of blissfulness.

An individual gains knowledge from scriptures; practices tapasya, meditation, and self-control without compulsion or expectation; and dives into an extraordinary experience of divine bliss. Since needs and carvings are at the minimum threshold, it teaches restraints and discipline to act ethically, thoughtfully, and meticulously. Parikrama helps an individual experience the presence of the Divine. Difficult terrain/situation contributes to shorn limitations of the mind, body, and carving. It helps to form a habit of staying in bliss continuously.

My father helped me take initial baby steps on the spiritual path. He enrolled me in the 'Bal Vihar' when I was around eight and also encouraged me to attend spiritual discourses. I studied scriptures, a source of valid written knowledge (sabda pramana) in praise of Gods, Deities and spiritual experiences of great Sages and Rishis. I grabbed opportunities to attend Satsang (spiritual discussions by learned authorities) to gain practical discipline and training in spiritual knowledge (Brahma Jyana). I understood the scriptures somewhat but needed special experiences (anubhava).

For a long time, I was in deep illusion through twists and turns, escalation and dives and consequences of my action and the surroundings. Within myself, I became inquisitive; if a combination of two energies can give birth to a child, then acquiring spiritual knowledge and my dedication to walk on the path can also liberate me from the cycle of birth and death. While on my journey towards self-realisation, I grappled with two profound questions. First, 'Who am I?' and second, 'considering I am an extension of the Divine through His manifestation, how can I unearth the Divine-like qualities within me, akin to extracting a diamond from a mine, and reveal them to myself?' My search for a satisfactory answer remained unfulfilled, and this quest to understand myself, ultimately led me to embark on the Narmada Parikrama.

> OM Peace, Peace, Peace
> Narmade Har.

Narmada

"What mind-dazzling views does nature gift us? The beauty of forests is unparalleled, and the view of rivers is even more charming. Where forests, mountains, rivers, or even the confluence of rivers meet in one place, nature exposes itself and gives a dance-like appearance. The joy of natural beauty gifts is unmatched. A person, who worries about his house, family and relatives, wealth and riches, land and property, wife and kids only, cannot see this beauty even if he looks at it. He stays blind in his worries. Those who do not care for any mundane matter, those whom God has planted detachment from worldly affairs in their hearts, only get fascinated by nature's beauty. In them grows the desire to always live with views like that, live in such places, and stay forever. On the banks of the Narmada, there are numerous locations like this."

Omkaranand Giri

Rivers have special significance; their contribution to economic and cultural development is vital. The density of population and agricultural cultivation is highest along the river banks. Due to waterways trade, commercial and spiritual centres have sprung up alongside rivers. From the distant past, four rivers in India have associations with the four Vedas, Rig Veda to Ganga, Yajur Veda to the Yamuna, Athara Veda to Saraswati, and Sam Veda to Narmada. The

Narmada River is indeed one of the five holiest sacred rivers alongside Ganga, Yamuna, Godavari, and Kaveri. As per Padma Purana, bathing in the waters of Yamuna purifies a man in seven days, in the waters of the Saraswati in three, and in the waters of the Ganges in one. However, Narmada purifies an individual with her single sight.

For this reason, people regard Narmada River (locally called Mai) as the most respectful and endearing mother. Hills, forests, barren land, and fertile fields stretch miles along the river. From a Geo-scientific point of view, the Narmada River Valley is 60 to 250 million years old. The Narmada has a unique position geographically, ecologically, and environmentally apart from having an economic impact on the lives of the region's people. The valley forms a separate geographical and cultural unit unique in its peculiar geological makeup.

Situated in a core earthquake zone, the Narmada River lies in a rift valley formed by basaltic flows. About 32% of the basin is forest, 45% is the net sown area, and 23% is barren. The average annual rainfall in the basin is 1178 mm. 90% of water comes during the monsoon months (June to September). The river's source is the Vindhya Mountains of Amarkantak, a basalt rock ridge with water-retaining properties released through a drip mechanism. The river moves over the states of Madhya Pradesh (81%), Gujarat (12%), Maharashtra (4%) and Chhattisgarh (2%). The river's flow area is approximately 36000 square miles, and the basin extends over 98,796 sq. Km.

The Narmada River springs from a kund in Amarkantak in Maikal hills, between the Vindhya and the Satpura range, at around 3500 feet above sea level. Together with her adjoining rivers, Tapti (South) and Mahi (North),

Narmada is one of three east-west rivers of peninsular India. Her origin is from Amarkantak hills, and travelling a distance of around 1312 kilometres, she merges in the Gulf of Khambhat in Bharuch. River Narmada flows through Chhattisgarh, Madhya Pradesh, Maharashtra and Gujarat. She covers districts of Shahdol, Chhattisgarh, Dindori, Mandala, Shivini, Jabalpur, Narsinghpur, Hosangabad, Harda, Khandwa, Khargoan, Badwani, Nandubar, Narmada, Bharuch, Vadodara, Alirajpur, Dewas, Sihor, Raisen, and Anuppur.

The Narmada basin has rich fauna and lush flora with an overall catchment area of about 98,800 kilometres. The Narmada flows through the mountain ranges of Vindhya in the North and Satpura in the South, which serves as an extensive watershed and represents a highly complex hydrological system. The river gets water through many rivers and rivulets from these mountain ranges. It has forty-one principal tributaries, twenty-two joining her on the south bank and 19 on the North (right) bank. Narmada Mahatmya describes 116 tributaries, with 61 confluences on the north and 55 on the South bank. The Narmada is geologically 150 million years older than the river Ganges.

The basin has five well-defined physiographic regions. It rises in the North-Eastern upland from Amarkantak (Maikal) range, primarily set off by massive rock formations.

1. The upper hilly areas cover the Shahdol, Mandla, Durg, Balaghat and Seoni districts.

2. The upper plains cover the Jabalpur, Narsinghpur, Sagar, Damoh, Chhindwara, Hosangabad, Betul, Raisen and Sehore districts.

3. The middle plains cover the districts of Khandwa, part of Khargone, Dewas, Indore, and Dhar.

4. The lower hilly areas cover the west Nimar, Jhabua, Dhulia, Narmada, and Vadodara.

5. The lower plains cover mainly the districts of Narmada, Bharuch, and parts of Vadodara.

Besides having many natural resources, Narmada is the basis of the public's spiritual and religious beliefs. It has a vast fertile field in its flow area, which is of significant importance from a social, literary, cultural, and economic perspective. Besides ensuring drinking water supply to cities on its banks, it contributes significantly to agriculture, tourism, and industries. Pilgrimages and spiritual places developed on its banks form a unique part of the Indian social system. Dams and river projects fulfil the state's electricity, water, and agriculture requirements. The impact of multi-purpose dams, irrigation, and hydel projects bears favourable fruits in Madhya Pradesh, Gujarat, Maharashtra, and Rajasthan. The Narmada, along with its tributaries, is the perennial source of irrigation in an extensive area. The main crops grown along the basin of Narmada are paddy, sugarcane, pulses, oilseeds, potatoes, wheat, and cotton, the primary food source in this area. Many fish species live in the river, and fishing activity thrives. Estimates of the annual water flow of the Narmada differ considerably, from 27,408 to 40,705 million cubic meters.

The ongoing progress of large-scale construction, population growth, deforestation, and mining is dramatic. Resettlement and rehabilitation for many people are happening whose houses are submerged or threatened due to major dams - Sardar Sarovar, Maheswar, Indira Sagar, Omkareshwar, and Bargi. It is changing the culture and landscape of the valley. Due to the depletion of the forest, irregular rainfall pattern has become the norm. In 2017 Madhya Pradesh received 27.69% less than the average rainfall affecting 97% of Narmada's catchment area. The entire Narmada valley, including the Vindhya Mountains of Amarkantak, must be preserved to ensure the perennial water flow into the river since policies do not decide how much water the river has to give. The river does.

The isolation of the valley and the relative inaccessibility of the surrounding terrain have limited the settlement of many people for a long time and hence became a perfect abode for Rishis and Munis.

Presence of Lord Brahma, Lord Vishnu, and Lord Shiva in the river body provides Narmada with a protective shield. Moreover, lakhs of visible and invisible celestial beings, like kinnara (musicians), amaras (devas), Rishis and Munis, worship the Narmada River.

Along her banks, Lord Vishnu, Brahma, Shiva, Pandavas, Rishi Maikala, Vyasa, Bhrigu, Kapila, Mrikandu, Markandey, Shaunaka, Devas, Vashistha, Sista, Pippala, Kardama, Sanatkumar, Nicheketa, Kashyap, Shankaracharya, Kabir and the like have taken refuge and done penance (tapasya). Sadhus, brahmacharis, and grihastha (ordinary individuals) undertake this arduous journey. They spend years on their spiritual journey to fulfil their respective individual ends, to be free from the shackles of this world by walking along its bank in a clockwise circular manner on foot, from one point to the end and back.

In mythological literature, the eastern or mountainous part of the river is called Rewa (playful). The western part is called Narmada (soft or giving happiness). The Rewa

Khanda chapter of Vayu / Skanda Purana and Narmada Mahatmya myths and legends connected with tirthas has a detailed narration. It describes the significance of holy places, temples, appropriate rites, and austerities for observation. Merits gained by such actions are therein. Narmada is in 23 verses of the Valmiki Ramayana, on 15 occurrences in the Mahabharata, and in works of Kalidasa and Raghuvamsa. In Matsya Purana, Padma Purana, and Kurma Purana, there are descriptions of the significance and pilgrimages of the Narmada. Narmada River is one of the sacred rivers and a goddess.

There are many Holy places of pilgrimage along the river Narmada, where many devotees come regularly. On the Southern bank, places of spiritual importance are - Mai ki Bagia, Kabir Chabutra, Gorakhpur, Dindori, Dev Gaon, Bargi Colony, Dhunadhar, Bhramakund, Budh Ghat, Saptdhara, Narmadapur (Hosangabad), Jaloda, Handia, Omkareshwar, Godhari Ghat, Shaliwahan, Raj Ghat, Gora Colony, Prakasha, Shuklatirth, Dhandeshwar, Mangrol, Hanumateshwar, Neelkanth, Poicha, Sukhdev, Koteshwar, Sisodhara, Gow Ghat, Maninareshwar, Bhalod, Gumandeva, Samor, Ankleshwar, Bulbula Kund and Bimleshwar where the Narmada merges into the sea. On the Northern bank, places of spiritual importance are – Mithi Talia, Lakhi Gaon, Koliad, Amleshwar, Bharuch, Jhadeshwar, Mangaleshwar, Angareshwar, Ambali, Ansuiya Mata, Koteshwar, Tilakwada, Maninareshwar, Garudeshwar, Hapeashwar, Warda, Ridheshwar, Mandawgarh (Mandu) Maheswar, Madleshwar, Bimleshwar, Kothawa, Nemawar, Anwari Ghat, Barman Ghat (Bhraman Gaht), Bhera Ghat, Ram Nagar, Mandala, Kapildhara, and Amarkantak.

People believe that after death, the individual's soul

attains salvation by immersing the body's ash in Narmada's water. Thus, people desire to have their last breath in her lap to achieve moksha (liberation from birth and death). Today, many famous ashrams and temples are along the river banks, where people worship and meditate. People organise many festivals and fairs on auspicious days. In many Shiva temples, Narmadeshwar Shivling, taken from the bed of the divine river, is installed.

Sages requested King Pururva that the holy Narmada would liberate the world from its sins and asked the King to find out how the Narmada could descend to Earth. King Pururva did an austere (tapasya) to please Shiva, and being pleased by his tapasya; Lord Shiva appeared before him. Pururva expressed his wish. Lord Shiva requested Narmada to descend to Earth. He instructed Paryank, son of Vindhyachal Mountain, to hold Narmada as she landed. Accordingly, Narmada came down on Earth as a pious River. Narmada blessed Pururva and instructed him to perform the tarpan rituals in the name of his ancestors to liberate them from their sins. Pururva complied, and thus by performing tarpan, liberated all his ancestors. Sage Markandeya, in his discourse to Yudhisthira, narrated that an individual who takes a holy dip in the Narmada attains virtues similar to performing Ashwamedh Yagya.

As per another mythological story, Lord Shiva performed extensive tapasya with Uma in Amarkantak Mountains for the welfare of the whole world. As the Lord was in tapasya, perspiration and sweat from his body flooded Amarkantak Mountain, and a river was born of it. In the first Krtayuga, she assumed a woman's form and worshipped Rudra (Lord Shiva) for ten thousand years. Being extremely happy, Lord Shiva, accompanied by Uma, asked Narmada for her wish. Narmada requested the Lord to let her be holy, imperishable, and well-known in all three worlds as the destroyer of great sins. Devotees who bathe in the Narmada River to get purified and acquire merit usually by taking a holy dip in all the tirthas of the Earth. The benefits of studying Vedas, doing the yagya, and giving daan (charity), are equivalent to a bath in the Narmada River. Let every living being that dies in her water go to Amravati, irrespective of their good or ignoble karmas, to have mental calmness with full control over their sense organs. She also desired that Lord Shiva always resides on her banks along with Uma (Parvati) and other deities adorning the Lord to attain moksha. Lord Shiva gave Narmada the boon that her devotees would get liberated from all their sins. Gods will live on her Northern bank along with Vishnu, Brahma, Indra, Chandra, Varuna, and Sadhaks. Lord Shiva and Uma, Pitras, will stay on the Southern bank accompanied by groups of Sages, Siddhas, Sutras, and Asuras.

King Manu was the ruler of Ayodhya during Swayambhuva Manvantar. Inspired by Sage Vashishth, Manu and his people went to Tripurari on the Narmada bank, took a holy dip, and got liberated. Sage Manu wanted to bring the sacred Ganga (River Ganges) and other holy rivers to Earth. So Manu performed a grand yagna on the bank of river Narmada and invited all the Sages and hermits. Seeing the devotion of Sage Manu, Narmada Mai blessed him and said. "In the first half of treyata yuga, one of your descendants, Bhagirath, would accomplish this great feat of bringing down the holy Ganga to Earth. In the second half of the same era, other sacred rivers like Kalindi, Saraswati, Sarayu, and Mahabhaga would also manifest."

Every stone found in the Narmada bed represents

Shiva Lingams. If placed in an appropriate place, the stone from the river is considered living Shiva Tirtha. It does not require the cosmos' ritual or divine vital energy to infuse life into the stone (prana pratistha). Rishis and Sanyasis found many secluded place on the Narmada bank with the least disturbances to complete their tapasya.

Circumambulation (circular journey) around Narmada Mai is known as Narmada Parikrama. An individual taking parikrama is known as parikramawasi. People carry out parikrama with great effort. Parikramawasi carries only the most essential requirements, such as clothes, a water pot, and a stick (Vyasa Danda).

Rishi Vyasa, son of Rishi Parashara, decided to have yagna in his Ashram on the southern bank of river Narmada. Many Sages and Munis came to attend the yagna. The Southern Bank of Narmada is for dedication to Pitras (ancestors), and the North Bank is devoted to Gods. When Rishi Parashara realised the Ashram was on the southern bank, he went to Rishi Vyasa. He told him Rishis and Munis would not accept his yagna due to the location of the Ashram. On hearing this, Rishi Vyasa told Rishi Parashara to wait for some time. Then, he went to Narmada Mai and prayed to her. After the prayer, he requested her to change her path. Initially, she refused to flow in the opposite direction. Rishi Vyasa was firm and told Narmada Mai that Rishis and Munis would not accept the yagna since the Ashram is on the southern bank of Narmada. Narmada Mai succumbed to the wishes of her child Rishi Vyasa and requested him to lead the way, and she would follow.

Rishi Vyasa had a stick in his hand, and he started to mark the path, and Narmada Mai followed the marking and changed her direction. All Rishi and Munis in attendance became happy, bathed in the Narmada, and accepted the offering of the yagna. The Ashram of Rishi Vyasa was in Mandla, where Narmada flows in a circular phase. In remembrance of Rishi Vyasa, the stick in the hand of all parikramawasi is Vyasa Danda. While taking sankalpa, after puja of the stick, it becomes Vyasa Danda. It shows the way to all parikramawasi. Parikramawasi offers prayers to Vyasa Danda daily and takes them to their home after their parikrama since it acts as a guiding force to lead their life.

Ashrams, temples, and people residing on the river banks usually provide food and shelter to parikramawasi. Parikramawasi sometimes sleeps by the roadside or under the shade of a tree or open sky. A bellyful meal, at times, is also nectar (amrita).

Upon completing parikrama, an individual must pay gratitude to Narmada Mai, Lord Omkareshwar, and Lord Mamleshwar. In Omkareshwar, parikramawasis offer puja (prayer) and abhishek (ordination) with Narmada water they had been carrying throughout the parikrama. After the puja, they do parikrama on Manhata (also known as Shivpuri) island, the shape of which is like OM. An invitation is being extended to Kanya (girl child less than twelve years), Saints and Brahmins to take prasad. The cooking of prasad (food and halwa) is in ghee. Kanya and Brahmins are worshipped before and then offered prasad. After prasad, all the invited people get dakshina (token donations); they bless them in return. Finally, back home, parikramawasi must shave their head and beard, perform Satyanarayan Puja, and enjoy a blessed life.

OM Peace, Peace, Peace

Narmade Har.

Foundation

The world consists of mainly unethical acts, sinful deeds and a lack of moral values. People are insecure. Often we cannot trust even our most trusted families and friends. Society is critical of Saints due to inappropriate and unethical conduct, arrogance, trading of their knowledge, and moving away from spirituality by a few individuals under the robe of a Saint. Through their behaviour, so-called Saints undermine the importance of holy places and indulge in criminal actions. Saints preach to their devotees to live a plain and simple life, but they indulge in affluence. People indulge in gambling and intoxication and take the opportunity to grab others' wealth by deceitful means. Married couples need to fulfil their obligation towards their partners, which many fail to adhere to. Treachery, hostility, and disrespect towards elders are on the rise.

Before starting for Narmada Parikrama, one has to examine the favourable position of the Moon in their astrological chart. I enquired about the same from a renowned Astrologer who said that from 9th January 2019, the Moon would be in a good position in my astrological chart. However, Rahu's and Ketu's situations were unfavourable till January 2021. I needed to avoid long journeys since I would likely face severe accidents or health issues. The inner calling of Narmada Parikrama was very compelling. Despite intense pain in the knees and warning from good wishers, I planned to start my journey on 15th January 2019, an auspicious day, Makar Sankranti. I, my elder sister Mrs Sudha Jha, my wife, Neeru Mishra, and my daughter Miss Maithili Mishra, started for Ujjain by Avantika Express, leaving Borivali Railway Station around 7.45 pm.

During the journey, I met a Saint exuding an aura of Divine tranquility. We started discussing the importance of Narmada Parikrama and its relevance in unveiling our true nature. According to him, we are pure consciousness (Atma). The body is an instrument governed by the mind, intellect, and ego. We are mostly driven outwardly in the arena of this world. At the same time, inwardness is necessary to understand your true self. I asked for his blessings, and he gently made me undergo a guided meditation. Alas, I went into a deep trance and saw a glimpse of parikrama. I bowed down, respected His Holiness, and returned to my berth.

My parents joined us in Ujjain. Ujjain is known for having numerous temples of different eras. On the bank of Shipra River, the world's largest spiritual gathering, Kumbha Mela (fair), occurs once in twelve years. During Mahabharata, Avantika (now Ujjain) was also a renowned learning centre. Lord Krishna, his brother Balarama, and his friend Sudama studied in a Gurukul (School) under Maharishi Sandipani. The Ashram has a divine atmosphere.

At Mahakaleshwar Temple I had darshan of Lord Shiva and felt blessed. A strange sight came as a shock to me. I saw a six-foot-tall handsome individual wearing a spotless ironed dhoti kurta (Indian Dress) with a long beard and silver hair up to the shoulder, decked up with an expensive diamond ring in his right hand, Rolex watch on his wrist, well-crafted gold chain with rudraksha beads performing Rudra Abhishek ceremony with twelve priests. During the entire ceremony, tears were rolling down from his eyes. After the spiritual ceremony, he still cried while distributing prasad to all the bhakts (devotees). Out of curiosity, I watched him, did Namaste, and inquisitively asked him why he was sad.

He said he worked around sixteen hours daily without any breaks for the last forty years. For professional work, he travelled across the globe and often missed his meals and necessities for the upliftment and decent living of the family. He took his family around the world during his assignments. They stayed in the best hotels. He made arrangements for their holidays while completing his projects. By the grace of God, he has enough wealth for himself and his family, the best cars, a beautiful Temple, houses in major cities, and adequate staff to care for their comfortable living. He had been grooming his son to take over his empire. His son declared that he felt clogged living with his parents and, from last year, started working in a company, left all the luxuries and was staying in a separate two-bedroom flat. Lately, his wife had also begun to complain that throughout their married life, he had ignored her and accused him of committing himself to only creating wealth and gaining fame at the expense of the family. She even blamed him for not spending quality time with her and their son. She has started living separately.

He was extremely upset and sad since he had spent his entire life creating wealth for his family and ensuring they had a luxurious living. Now, his wife and son blamed him for ignoring them and have left him alone. Hearing his story, I got a little perturbed seeing what happens when we do not live a balanced life. In the past, I have heard many cases of this kind. The person had put in his best effort to create a financial empire for his family. However, he should have included other vital aspects necessary for family bonding and cordial relationships. When he required the family by his side, they left him. Is this the reward for the hard work?

From the Mandir, I came to the hotel. My family members were ready and waiting for me to take them for a darshan of Mahakaleshwar Mahadev. My mother was unable to walk. Therefore, I arranged for an attendant and a wheelchair to ferry her to the Mandir (Temple), and my father, sister, wife, and daughter walked to the Temple for darshan. All of us had a memorable and blissful darshan. After the darshan, we sat in the hall for some time. We again went to the Mandir the next morning to offer puja and take blessings. After performing puja at Mahakaleshwar Mahadev Temple and local sightseeing, we proceeded to Omkareshwar.

In Omkareshwar, we stayed at Gajanan Maharaj Ashram. By the grace of God, I had the darshan of a Saint from the Himalayas who had come to pay homage to Narmada Mai. He had an athletic build, a Divine glow on his face, beautiful lengthy deadlocks, and magnetic eyes. After the salutation, I asked Swami Ji – What is the cause of frustration and unhappiness, and why do good people suffer?

He said an individual needs to have four aligned life purposes and comprehensively spend their focus and energy to remain successful and happy. The first purpose is to observe Dharma – to be ethical with self, nature, and society and lead the right way of living. The second is Artha - pursue material prosperity (including health, finances, education, family, status, career, and networks) through serving humanity and the Divine. The third is karma – satisfaction and happiness while pursuing ethical passion, responsibilities, and duties. The last one is moksha - spiritual liberation and salvation. Unfortunately, today's primary focus of life is towards growth in occupation and wealth creation. Many individuals ignore their health, family, social obligations, ethics, passion, and spiritual growth to peruse their careers or business. It is challenging to satisfy the self with external (including financial) desires, which leads to emptiness and, in turn, leads to frustration and unhappiness.

He further informed me that I would understand the illusion of 'good people' and 'suffering' at an appropriate time during parikrama. I will get a proper explanation for the question, 'Why do good people suffer.' I requested him to enlighten me on the path to success and happiness. He elaborated that life can be bifurcated roughly into two phases. In the first phase of life, an infant moves from childhood to career, marriage, family, lifestyle, and community networking. This phase focuses on acquiring worldly knowledge and skills, serving society, earning, maintaining a family, and living a desired lifestyle. Be socially connected, accept rewards, and self-actualise in his chosen field. In the second sphere, the focus turns inside to attain moksha, ultimate and permanent happiness.

In the formative stage, from birth to around six years, life revolves primarily around developing the child's values through love, care, compassion, play, physical growth, understanding self-discipline, social norms, religion and spiritual values. The focus of attention is on the child.

From six to thirteen years, the child starts moving out of the comfort of his home and interacts with nature and his primary community of home, school, friends, relatives, customs and religion. Learning intellectual and social skills, playing group games, and imbibing social and self-discipline takes over. Living ethical and societal values, eating, and physical growth likes and dislikes is their area of focus. During this stage, the child gets a fair idea of his passions, likes and dislikes, and weaknesses. Parents start imposing their visions of an ideal child and expect them to deliver results accordingly. The focus shifts to education and skill-building from thirteen to around twenty-six years. An individual starts preparation for employment, career, marriage, and family. The core building stage of the first sphere is known as Brahmacharya (student age).

Nature has all shades of colour, and God has given many career and occupational shades that complement society. You will never see a neem leaf in a mango tree; similarly, an individual will never be satisfied and happy if they don't pursue their area of passion and interest. The fruit becomes unpleasant when they try to tweak their career in areas of their dislike. Parents try to manipulate the child's occupation based on self and societal expectations, which creates unhappiness in the long run.

From twenty-six years to around sixty-five years, adults spend time pursuing their passion, career, lifestyle, and other areas of interest, managing their families and children. Emphasis is on serving society, wealth creation, social networking, having their own family, ensuring proper growth of their kids, and being successful in their desired domain. When an individual's life is spiritually, intellectually, mentally, emotionally, and physically aligned, success and happiness rein; otherwise, dissatisfaction brings stress, misery, and disease.

Interestingly, one stage of life leads to a higher set over time. Every stage of life has unique characteristics, considered acceptable and rewarded for achievement. However, moving to the next step, one must shun earlier good behaviour and adapt to what is adequate for that stage; otherwise, they get criticised and punished.

By the time one reaches sixty-five years, children grow up, are married, and start living their own lives. The responsibility of the first sphere ends, and it is time to stop interfering with others' experiences (including their own near and dear ones). It is only logical that after completing their family and career responsibilities, an individual must gradually withdraw from routine and shift their focus from the action of the outer world to self-retrospection, i.e., energising internal movement. In the first stage of this sphere, an individual need to prepare to renounce physical, material, and sexual pleasures. On retirement from his social and professional life, he should spend time with the Divine or in his work selflessly. With continuous practice, slowly and steadily, an individual's internal energy forces start aligning with the superior forces. As this happens, individuals can renounce all desires, fears, hopes, duties, and responsibilities and spend time in total devotion to God. This path leads to lasting happiness and bliss. It helps individuals virtually merge with God attaining moksha (release from the circle of birth and death).

A rope is enough to hold a Calf (baby elephant) when they are young, which they cannot break free. They try breaking the cord but cannot set themselves free due to a lack of strength. Their mind gets conditioned to the idea that they do not have the power to break the rope. As the elephants grow up, they can easily break the cord with strength. However, they do not even try to set themselves free due to their conditioned mind. They believe the rope holds them throughout their life, so they never try to break free. We, as individuals, get hooked on certain limiting beliefs imposed by society, especially during our formative childhood stages. As we learn and grow, the limiting beliefs restrict us from attaining our unlimited potential.

I asked the Saint, who can guide me to find my higher purpose, show me the path, and hold me through the grind to achieve the same? He replied, "Have faith in Narmada Mai; immerse yourself in parikrama. She will unveil your real purpose and assist you in walking on the path of self-realisation.

A short but powerful message opened a pandora's box, as teachings and behaviour of life showed excessive spending of our energy knowingly or unknowingly for worldly leisure and pleasures. So I started pondering on my quest to understand "Who am I" and "What is my purpose in this lifetime"? Is it the linear stages of life starting from education to occupation to getting married and taking care of children? I asked myself - moving further, should I waste my energy to earn wealth and enjoy worldly luxuries, or should I commit to the higher call? The Saint's message was loud and clear. To excel, I have to break away from self-limiting beliefs. Irrespective of the challenges, I need to have a positive self-image and a "can-do attitude", act to the best of my ability and put 100% effort into completing the spiritual task.

On 17th January 2019, I performed a puja at Omkareshwar Temple on Manhata Island at the Sangam (confluence) of the Narmada and Kaveri rivers. My sister, wife, daughter, and I did a parikrama of OM-shaped Omkareshwar Mountain in the afternoon. We were fortunate to have an elaborate Kanya Bhojan ritual in the evening, followed by darshan and puja at Mamleshwar Temple.

I bathed in the Narmada Mai (river) the next morning after the mundan (tonsure). Anusthan is a deliberate undertaking for a definite period with accepted yama (restraints) and niyama (regulations) for purifying the self. As a parikramawasi, I needed to strictly restrain myself from shaving, haircut, trimming nails and applying soap. While bathing in the Narmada, I could not use soap or oil. I had to control my physical needs, strictly obey complete celibacy, and observe the rules of Brahmacharya. It was mandatory to bathe daily, preferably in Narmada Mai, perform prayers, aarti, and sadhana in the morning and evening, attend satsang as often as possible, and drink Narmada water wherever possible. I could not cross the Narmada River or go to any of her islands. However, I could pass Narmada's tributaries only once at the respective confluences. While walking, I had to keep river Narmada to the right, recite mantras like Narmade Har, OM Namah Shiva and remain happy.

I started the rituals of Anusthan (ceremony) for Narmada Parikrama. I took water in hand and, after taking Sankalpa (resolution), offered it to the Earth, signifying a promise to complete the parikrama as per norms. Sankalpa continually reminded me of the goal, objectives, expectations, specific conditions, requisite material, and processes. Every day, repetition of the same sankalpa ensures that the purposes remain firm and clear. The idea of achievements and commitments remains consistent. It creates awareness and opportunity for introspection. A lengthy project like Narmada Parikrama also provides an opportunity for self-correction.

After sankalpa, puja started with the dhyana of Narmada Mai by reciting shlokas and avahan (appeal to Goddess Narmada) with a request to come and remain present at the place of worship. I washed Narmada Mai's feet with water, smeared her with sandal paste and kumkum, and offered flowers, prasad, dhoop, and deep. After that, I did aarti, pradakshina, and yachana to complete Narmada Parikrama and requested for the pardon of my flaws. I finally bowed down to obtain blessings of Narmada Mai - the giver of liberation, happiness and joy, remover of sins and destroyer of the cycle of birth and death.

Around noon, I started my Parikrama from Gomukh Ghat, Omkareshwar. I walked to Mortakka (12 kilometres) on the tar road. This patch worked as a training ground to test my fitness and readiness for the future journey. At Jagreshwar Mahadev Mandir, Mortakka, I listened to a Saint's exciting and useful discourse stating that with limited knowledge, you attract what seems right or hate what you dislike. Attraction and aversion create bondages/restrictions responsible for so-called happiness or misery. Satisfaction from worldly pleasure is temporary with strings attached. It enhances stress, body imbalance, blood pressure, weak immune system, fatigue, sleeping disorder, depression, conflict, and health declines over time. However, bliss comes from knowledge of permanent reality. The supreme is responsible for all the creations, and he is the creator. In the real sense, you are your Atma (consciousness).

He went on - those who practice spiritualism without restraints and regulations are fools. Observing restrictions and limitations allows you to enjoy a free flow of trust, love, and affection. Blessing of Narmada Mai will enhance your awareness, boost your energy and vibration, and reduce negativity, anger, and hatred. With pure energy, spiritual knowledge, tranquillity, and understanding, your attention will move from outer attraction to inner self. With a one-pointed focus on self-realisation and sadhana over time, you will connect deeper within. The veil of Maya will unfold; permanent joy from Atma (consciousness) will be a new reality, which is your true self.

After the satsang, I sat down alone and tried to unwrap myself. I got submerged in thoughts and past experiences, especially negative ones. Mortakka onwards, the path was uneven along the bank of Narmada Mai. I started my journey navigating through rough and, at times, tedious paths with many small, medium, and big pebbles, stones, and trenches caused by tires of overloaded tractors used for sand mining. I was not used to nor practised walking on uneven roads with fifteen kilograms of weight in a backpack on my shoulder. In my left hand, I held around two litres of water in my kamandal (container). I had Vyasa Danda (stick) in my right hand to balance myself. Due to continuous past negative thoughts, I got distracted and was unable to navigate the uneven path and trenches. I became fearful of falling and hurting myself. On a few occasions, I could save myself; however, a few hundred meters before Bari Ali, I had a fall. Water fell out of the container, my right knee twisted, and my leg pain became severe within a fraction of a minute. A Saint with long silver-white hair and a beard seeing me in pain rushed to my rescue. He carried my backpack, assisted me in crossing over the uneven patch, massaged my feet, gave me water to drink, and tried his best to console me that I would be fine.

In my mind, waves of disturbing thoughts started unfolding, creating fear, alarm and uncertainty about completing parikrama. The Saint advised me to remain calm and silence my mind. Rest in an Ashram, everything shall be all right, and you shall complete the parikrama. When I calmed down, he asked me how I fell, and I told him it was due to a lack of focus since my mind was busy with past negative experiences. He explained in a very soft tone that pulling yourself out of a self-created negative spiral, panic, anxiety, and uncertainty is difficult. He asked me to keep a strict disciplinary approach, be mentally positive, and have faith in Narmada Mai. He blessed me and wished me an early recovery.

In an hour, as I regained my confidence, the Saint escorted me to Narmada Ashram, Bari Ali. Mata Ji at Ashram showed motherly compassion. She gave me a glass of milk with turmeric powder and reassured me that my pain would subside and I could complete my parikrama. Mata Ji instructed me to be calm, put ointment around my knees, and rest. She suggested that after taking a bath the next day, to have a darshan of Baba Garib Das Ji ki Samadhi (Her Guru and father) and share my problem. Your knee will be all right - a ray of hope made me happy. After that, inside the covered verandah, I took a nap.

At night, I started analysing the reason for my fall. Despite my positive outlook, I still had considerable negativity due to past experiences. My elder daughter Maithili, a sportswoman, often reminded me that in competitive sports, endurance and rate of failure are extremely high. Individuals practice for years to win an important event. The negativity of the outer world, laden with fear, ego, anxiety, jealousy, distraction and stress, pulls an individual down, especially during the most critical times. To overcome failure, they practice meditation and creative visualisation. It makes them grounded and strong. They imagine success daily for years to take control of the mind under stress. An insight flashed that the only way to get out of this downward spiral is to be aware of my thoughts and beliefs, drop harmful internal dialogue immediately, perceive positivity within the experience and make the necessary corrections. Around 8.00 pm, Mata Ji gave me five chapattis and vegetables to eat. After dinner, I washed my plates, and after that, I did my meditation, puja, and aarti and went to sleep. Despite the pain, I had a sound sleep. The next morning, I gathered courage and vowed to be positive and continue my parikrama. I managed to climb down the stairs to Narmada Mai and bathed. Climbing up, I went straight to Baba Garib Das ki Samadhi.

At the Samadhi, I envisioned different shades of the Divinity of Narmada Mai in her creation. The fall, with a heavy load on my shoulders, was capable of causing serious health issues. In a very subtle way, Narmada Mai took care of my negative samskaras with a very light punishment. A flashback reminded me that after night comes a day, and after that night, again. In a natural life cycle, winning and hardship are part and parcel. Life is full of struggles, capable of throwing obstacles in the way; however, within the battle, opportunities are hidden. I realised that I am more powerful than any struggle and can overcome the same. It boosted my confidence and energy. I learned my lessons - focus on my purpose, be neutral to the results of actions, seek blessings of Mai, and appropriate assistance will come at the right time. With renewed self-confidence and energy, I prepared to continue my journey.

On my return to the Ashram, she gave me a glass of milk with turmeric powder and a photo of Narmada Mai along with chunri (stoal), sindoor (vermilion), chandan (sandalwood powder), bati (cotton twig), and a small copper vessel for aarti. She taught me the correct procedure to perform puja and aarti. She instructed me to always keep the idol/ photo of Narmada Mai and Narmada water in a saffron cloth since it is the colour of Agni (fire), symbolising the Supreme Being. Hindu Saints wear saffron robes as a mark of renunciation of material life. Ensure to clean the place before performing puja and spread a saffron cloth. Burn incense or a dia (lamp) since it is a distinct symbol of ancient Vedic rites to bring sattvic energy. Apply haldi (turmeric) and kumkum (powder used for religious markings). It is a sign of honour, concentration, strength, and prosperity. Before having food, offer naivedya (food offered to the Divine) to Narmada Mai.

Start puja by reciting OM as it emanates vital vibrations from the prana (consciousness) of the universe. OM (AUM) represents past, present, and future time respectively. It is the primordial sound, symbolic of the Brahman, and the sum of all the sounds that emanate from the human throat. "A" emerges from the throat, originating in the region of the navel (waking state), "U" rolls over the tongue (dreaming state), and "M" ends on the lips (sleeping state). After OM, perform 24 syllables Gayatri Mantra. Goddess Gayatri, also known as Veda-Mata or the mother of the Vedas (Rig, Yajur, Sama, and Atharva), can fulfil all the work ordained for you. She will keep you happy. The meaning of the mantra is - O Divine Mother, my heart is filled with darkness. Please make this darkness distant from me and promote illumination within me. After that, recite shlokas and Narmada Astak Bhajans, followed by Narmada aarti. Sit in meditation for some time. Pray for forgiveness, and after that, wrap the idol/photo and water of Narmada in saffron cloth and keep it in a clean and safe place.

She told me to observe fast on Purnima (Full Moon) and Amavasya (New Moon) as Moon significantly influences human anatomy. A person may become restless, irritable, and ill-tempered during this period. Fast helps restore the body and mind balance, reduces the acidic content in our system, slows the metabolic rate, and increases endurance. Prayer reinforces subduing emotions and controls the outburst of temper. I felt blessed to be with Mata Ji. I expressed my thanks for her blessings and motherly care.

After breakfast, as I was about to leave, a lady, parikramawasi, came to the Ashram. She had suffered from sciatica and was bedridden for seven years. She had taken sankalpa to do parikrama on foot or in a vehicle as appropriate since her husband was a patient with acute diabetes and blood pressure. Her son had come to Pune on a month's leave to care for his father. After serving tea and breakfast (balbhog), Mata Ji asked me to help her up to Gomukh Ashram.

We started our journey through the village road alongside Narmada Mai and came to Gomukh Ashram. This Ashram had a nursing home and a few guest rooms for parikramawasis. After showing our papers, we got separate guest rooms. After the darshan of Gautameshwar Mahadev, we had lunch and decided to take rest. Around 3.00 pm, we started for Rawer Kheri and, on the way, had afternoon snacks on the farm of Mr Radhey Shyam. He was a self-contained, well-built man with ethical virtues.

On his farm, he had a godown, a bedroom, cots, and a swing attached to mango trees. Farmers in this area have large parcels of land, usually five acres per plot. Water from Narmada takes care of irrigation. Cotton and wheat are the main crops grown in the area. During our discussion, he shared his willingness to donate his land for the service of parikramawasis if someone could manage the show.

The road to Rawer Kheri had lots of potholes. Bullock carts and motorcycles were ferrying goods and people. Seeing the condition of the lady parikramawasi, Mr Radhey Shyam arranged for a bike to drop her at the bus stand. I continued my parikrama and decided to stay in an Ashram at Rawer Kheri. In the Ashram, an old Sadhu with few followers had returned from Kumbh Mela, Allahabad. They were busy with spiritual discourse. According to them, spiritualism and religion have been an intrinsic part of society in India. For thousands of years, Vedas, Upanishads, Ramayana, Mahabharata, and other granths (spiritual books) have been a source of inspiration, comfort and relief to humanity.

During recent times, financial wealth, relationships, more than necessary wants, and undesired displays of wealth have taken too much time and attention. Outer achievements make it difficult for individuals to connect to their inner selves, a source of lasting happiness and peace. Money has become prominent, and people are busy amassing wealth, ethically or otherwise. It is the parameter of success. Stress, conflicts, depression, suicide, and divorce have increased many folds in society. Individuals need to practice self-restraint and regulate themselves to see the meaning of their life. Otherwise, they will be devoid of lasting peace and happiness. In the present culture, people will not be able to build trust, love, compassion, or harmony, nor will they be able to pay gratitude or pardon themselves or others, which is the glue to social happiness.

After the discourse, all of us got involved in preparing dinner. Well past midnight, I was tossing under my sleeping bag, trying to find out how to get to know my life's true meaning and walk on the spiritual path.

Sages have devoted their lives to finding and walking the path of eternal freedom. Pondering over last night's discussion, I visited Samadhi of Bajirao Peshwa the next morning, who served as General of the Maratha Empire. Moving ahead to Bakawa, I had to cross the Prawar River. The water level was up to shoulder level, and the rocks were slippery. I was struggling and praying to Narmada Mai to help me cross the river. Suddenly two parikramawasis came to the shore to cross the river to go forward. Seeing my indecisiveness, they left their belongings, took my backpack, and helped me cross the river. After that, they went back to fetch their baggage. After crossing the river, they told stories of how Siyaram Baba of Teli Bathyain has inspired people to live up to their higher self and build happiness and peace through spiritual practices. They narrated a few examples of how he had healed the community through spiritual practices.

To reach Bakawan, I had to climb a steep hillock at the bank of Narmada Mai. The village has Shiva and Balarama Temple and ruins of an old fort of Raja Mordh Raj. It is densely populated, with a school, a dispensary and a bus stand. The area has fertile black soil with water and irrigational facilities. Conventional crops grown in the region are wheat, cotton, chilly, soya bean, peanuts, and sugarcane. Bakawan is famous for the sculpture of Narmadeshwar

Shiva Lingas from the stones found in Narmada Mai and exporting them worldwide. I reached the village around 9.00 am and heard loud noises of machines cutting and polishing rocks. I went to a showroom displaying Shiva Lingas of multiple types, with costs ranging from five to more than one hundred thousand rupees. As I was crossing Bakawan, a bhakt called me to his house and gave me a glass of fresh milk and a packet of biscuits.

Ahead of Bakawan, the road was dusty, with many bushes along the path. The road had a deserted look, with not a soul around. Before reaching Mardana, an old skeletal lady suddenly appeared in the opposite direction. She had wrinkles around her face, was half bent from her waist, walked with the help of a stick, was wearing an old sari, and had scattered hairs. As she came close to me, I got frightened. I said Narmade Har, and in a very subtle voice, she reciprocated and said she was sick and wanted some money for treatment and medicine. I opened the front pocket of my backpack and gave her money, which I had received as donations along the way. She blessed me and moved forward. A moment later, I decided to give her some extra cash. As I turned back, she had disappeared by then, and I could not see her. I got scared and dragged myself to Bhatyan Teli with much courage. Later I heard such stories from other parikramawasis. According to them, it is a test to see one's compassion and love for humanity.

I felt blessed to have had a darshan of Saint Siyaram Baba in Bhatyan Teli, ninety-plus years old. Baba is a real example of compassion, care, and love above self. He is very active and wears only a loincloth all around the year. Baba did tapasya in the waters of Narmada Mai for twelve years and is considered a living deity due to his knowledge, spiritual energy, sacrifice, compassion, and love for all. He takes up to only ten rupees as dakshina (donation) and personally serves fruit prasad to all devotees. He is very fond of dogs; they roam around the room and share the same space with people in the Ashram. His Ashram is going to be submerged underwater; due to the construction of the Maheshwar Dam. He received twenty-four million rupees as compensation, which he donated to construct a Temple. He ensures that all the needs of parikramawasis are taken care of, like woollen blankets, puja items, ghee, clothes, ration and medicines. All bhakts were served wholesome food in sufficient quantity during lunch and dinner. I stayed in the Ashram for a day. I was blessed to enjoy the happiness and vibrations flowing out of Saint Siyaram Baba. Early morning all villagers in a procession did kirtan. They bathed in the Narmada and performed aarti at Hanuman Mandir.

I asked Baba how to attain self-realisation. He explained that the happenings of the world and the situation of your life are a theatre play. The outer world is the reflection of one's mind and emotions. Like an actor, perform worldly duties without getting attached to results thereof or substances or being swamped in desires. Be aware of Maya because temporary happiness is short-lived. Fulfilment of wishes does not give lasting satisfaction, and misery engulfs. God is not separate from you; you (Atma) are not different from yourself. He is the creator of energy in each karn (atom). Truth is pure, beautiful, mahakal (beyond time), omnipresent, not an object to be acquired or be known since he is infinite and beyond our comprehension. Since our Atma is an extension of the supreme, we can attain unlimited happiness if we know ourselves.

We receive worldly knowledge through the five sense organs, mind, intellect, and emotions. Our mind's nature repeatedly pops up negative experiences and memories, even though many good ones would have happened in the past. We perceive and tie ourselves to our memories from our previous and this life; limited intellect, emotions, knowledge; and the signals received through our five sense organs. We are neither intellect, emotions, nor organs; all of it is part of us. To overcome this limitedness, be aware of your surroundings, thoughts, and feeling; develop a witness attitude and talk to your inner self. It takes time to erase our memory, as we usually carry forward old feelings. We tend to mix past negative emotions with the present and miss out on new, neutral, or positive blessings and ideas. Be aware of yourself, your priorities, and your day, and spend time with your inner self. It helps you to identify yourself, bring positivity, and provide new spiritual awareness, rather than being a social animal and spending time in the world.

Time is a continuum of "now," and every moment of life is new. The unknown makes us more observant and provides a learning opportunity. With proficiency in worldly matters, our knowledge and alertness decreases. Being willing to learn is essential, live in the present, and look at a situation from a broader perspective. Every moment is new, and learning happens in newness. With a low level of energy, people get confused, lazy, talkative, and distracted. Enhance your enthusiasm and knowledge to find the truth and unveil the consciousness within. Eat sattvic food in small quantities. Be ethical, do sadhana, sewa, meditation, satsang, bhajan, asana, and pranayama to raise vitality and mindfulness for self-realisation. Practice, Practice, and Practice. With the power-packed lesson from Baba, my curiosity to know "Who am I" and my faith in fulfilling my objectives during Narmada Parikrama strengthened. The incidences of the last few days gave me confidence that Narmada Mai is taking care of me and my purpose. What a gift!

On introspection, to my surprise, I found only a handful of adverse situations or suffering made me feel miserable. I realised that suffering is a normal slice of our life cycle; however, our mind plays an active role in making us sad. The feeling of only a few betrayals generates anger within and diminishes the power of discrimination, leading to conflicts. The relationships of years crack in a flash of a moment and may take years to fill the gap.

During the parikrama, I spent a few days testing the power of negative emotions and situations, only to realise that I lost tremendous energy by imagining them. I must have replayed a few negative emotions so often in the past, only to form a habit of negativity and anger. I realised that the right thoughts and happy feelings gave me success. In contrast, negative beliefs and anger brought subsequent failures. Positive thoughts build energy within, whereas negativity drains energy. It took me some time to be aware of my thoughts and emotions, to look at a broader perspective, and to start living in the present. Subsequently, after that, parikrama took a new turn, and I started enjoying every moment. The scenic landscape along Narmada Mai became pleasing, where habitat, trees, bush, crocodiles, birds, and animals dance to the music of the flowing water.

OM Peace, Peace, Peace

Narmade Har.

Building Blocks

While walking along the banks of the river Narmada, I saw a large bird waiting patiently for her prey catching only big fish. She let go of the small fish, and when a large fish was within range, she grabbed it and flew to the shore. I observed her for about an hour and drew parallels with my life. What an astonishing way of working on clear priorities! I compared and pondered how we get over-involved in non-essential things and, in doing so, miss deadlines on the important ones. Roughly, an individual engages more than 70% of waking time on problems, tasks, or issues, which do not require their involvement. More importantly, it happens unknowingly due to habits despite our determination to avoid them. As a result, significant energy and resources get involved in non-purposeful and trivial issues. Energy flows in the direction where our focus goes. We must be aware of our purpose, passion, and single-minded focus on it like a laser beam to succeed. Otherwise, an individual misses life's real meaning, leading to unnecessary stress and frustration.

On the way to the Gordhari Ghat, there was a wrestling competition. Many young Saints were participating as well as coaching youngsters in the arena. My curiosity compelled me to know why Saints are interested in wrestling. An elderly Saint explained that the body is the Temple, and inside is the pure consciousness. The Temple needs to be in excellent condition to realise self-awareness. Health is wealth; therefore, be compassionate to yourself and maintain a healthy body. For a healthy body, it is essential to ethically restrain and regulate behaviour when interacting with the outside world and honour the happenings within the mind and emotions.

For disciplining sadhaks, akharas have a tradition of wrestling. In wrestling, the individual must follow discipline and stay healthy, alert, calm, composed, and focused. Today, we do not miss an opportunity to abuse ourselves and others. In the name of religion, people undertake multiple days of fasting in a week out of devotion or fear, irrespective of their health conditions. Fitness enthusiasts give importance to the body and weight maintenance at the cost of their long-term health. On the flip side are individuals who care least and abuse their bodies for sensory gains. Torturing, punishing, or giving shock to our body disturbs the sympathetic and para-sympathetic nerves, bringing dullness and sickness.

We have reached the pinnacle of intolerance. We do not even spare our near and dear ones if they do not align with our expectations. We don't even spare kids; we shout or punish them if they are playing or making noise when we are busy doing something important (maybe at their cost). Anger brewing within self gets an opportunity to project through someone else. Unregulated life causes an imbalance in the nervous system, causing weight gain, rift, agitation, blood pressure, diabetes, dullness, and other types of illness. Happiness flows out of a healthy system, and with it comes fulfilment. With joy comes love, peace, and harmony. Therefore, it is essential to restrain and regulate ourselves.

I asked the Saints to outline the steps an ordinary individual needs to follow to remain healthy. To stay healthy, an individual must have a higher purpose in life, appropriate physical, mental and emotional balance, and fitness throughout his life. I further asked - how can we attain this level of stability and fitness? Moderation and balance in quantity and quality of food, water, sleep, physical exercise, breathing and meditation are the keys. Eat sattvic food in the right amount at appropriate intervals. We advise our sadhaks (disciples) to avoid eating ready-to-eat or chemical food since they are tamasic or rajasic in nature. They make the mind wander in various directions. Light and fresh food create a light body and a more luminous mind.

An aspirant needs to have a life's purpose as it acts like the North Star. A person should always act ethically and restrain themselves from unnecessary desires. They must follow social regulations, exercise appropriately in the morning or evening, do pranayama (breathing exercises), and meditate for some time. Thus, like wrestlers, they will become physically fit, mentally calm, and emotionally composed. During the game of life, their living ensures that their physical stamina synchronises with breathing, mental calmness, and emotional determination. His words resounded in my mind, and I wanted to know more. He blessed me and told me to be aware of my surroundings and eliminate harmful internal dialogues. Learn from every being, follow the rules of parikrama, have faith in yourself and Narmada Mai, learn and keep a healthy style of life.

I felt blessed and started walking. As I passed Gordhari Ghat, a woman gave me ladoo prasad and blessed me - a sign of blessing from Narmada Mai. By lunchtime, I reached Ram Mandir, Lepa Ghat. While resting under a tree,

Mr Mangilal Verma came from his residence and escorted me to his home for lunch. His house was on the bank of the Narmada; it had a depleted look and required significant repairs. He had few cattle and a small piece of land on which the family survived. His family members prepared a wholesome lunch, which I enjoyed. After chatting for some time, I returned to the Temple and offered Mr Verma some money as gift for his kids, which he refused to accept, saying I would need it and Lord Ram took care of him.

By evening I reached Makad Khera and stayed in Shri Vedanta Vila Ashram. It was a well-developed Ashram spread around ten hectares with a distinctive landscape adjacent to the highway. Swami Ji of the Ashram succumbed to injuries in a car accident six months back. His family members are taking care of the Ashram. It has well-maintained Indian and Western toilets, separate bathing rooms, and washing areas. In the evening, I washed my clothes and, after dinner, spent some time gazing at the sky. Due to the Purnima (full moon night), the sky was clear with a congregation of stars and a reddish full Moon. In Mumbai, due to pollution, we seldom witness a clear sky.

The Next morning, after a hot water bath, I enjoyed a glass of milk. I walked along the bank of Narmada Mai to Ekadash Shivling, Kathora. While having the darshan, Baba Ji (Saint of the Ashram) enquired why I was wearing a kneecap. I replied that I was wearing a kneecap due to an injury. He told me to remove the kneecap and apply the therapeutic oil he had prepared on my knees. Within a few minutes, the pain reduced, and I started walking comfortably without a kneecap. Baba Ji comes from Amarkantak and makes medicinal oil with eleven herbs useful in joint pain. His mission is to distribute the oil, free of cost, to patients suffering from joint pains and arthritis. He also gave me a bottle of oil for my onward journey. I shared the medicinal oil with other needy parikramawasis, and they also experienced relief. Another miracle and my belief in Narmada Mai became well-grounded. We discussed the spiritual significance of leading a simple life when a disappointed student approached Baba Ji regarding the cause of his failure.

An intelligent, hardworking, studious student was confident to pass a competitive examination but could not succeed. Feeling dejected, he came to the Temple to offer prayers and seek an explanation from the Saint for the cause of his failure despite putting in his best. He inquisitively asked Baba Ji - why an individual should not expect favourable results when he has the potential to succeed and has given his best effort to pass the exam. Baba Ji replied that God created the universe and has provided all possible elements - earth, water, fire, air, and space. Our body down to an atom is the outcome of the combination and permutation of these elements. However, many environmental forces also influence our surroundings and energy equilibrium. Therefore, the appropriate application of our mental, intellectual, emotional, and physical effort is only partly accountable for results. We do not have control over many other factors of the environment. The results of an action are dependent on many different factors.

For example, wheat seed sowed in winter only in fertile land, not in a desert, will give the desired output. After sowing, the quality of the plant and the proceeds will depend on many other factors, some within reach and others beyond, such as quality of seed, soil, weather, water, fertiliser, etc. You can control your effort to sow and, to some extent, provide water, appropriate fertiliser, etc. However, if the area gets flooded and you do not get the required output, the weather is the cause of failure, not your effort. Therefore, the farmer will again put his energy into farming; otherwise, the inaction of not putting effort into agriculture will lead to poverty.

One has the right over his action but not the result because the result is a combination of several energies. It is an illusion that makes people believe that the doer is solely responsible for the development because energy combinations are responsible for the outcome. If the result is proportionate only through your efforts, positive results will make you egoistic, whereas adverse consequences will bring inaction, both having ill effects. Ego and inaction will not allow you to introspect, and that will stop your growth.

After the discussion, we had aloo (potato) paratha prepared by a lady parikramawasi, who came from Germany and was staying in the Ashram. After lunch, I asked the lady her purpose behind doing parikrama. She replied in India, she can establish a relationship within self and community, ecology, environment, and the Divine. She further elaborated that it is unbelievable to imagine the warmth shown to parikramawasis by people living on the banks of the Narmada Mai until one experiences it. Bhakt goes out of their way to serve and help without expectations. Their hospitality is far more compassionate than can be perceived. Nowhere in the world can anyone dream of venturing out on a parikrama for up to three years, three months and thirteen days without having a penny in their pocket and still being cared for all their needs more than their expectations.

While living in India, her awareness, connections,

relationships, and commitment to self-realisation and fulfilling her duties and obligations towards others have moved to a new level. She enjoys being peaceful in her new state of being. Every year she visits India and spends time in the Himalayas, Varanasi, and other spiritual places.

After lunch, I came to Shaliwahan Ghat. The Ashram has an ancient Temple of Lord Shiva, cottages for Saints, and a modern complex for parikramawasis. On the opposite (northern) bank of Narmada, the grandeur of Maheswar Ghat and Ahilya Bai Fort had a panoramic view with golden rays of sunrise enhancing the entire stretch. A few parikramawasis from Bharuch, Gujarat, also came to Shaliwahan. They were doing parikrama on foot; however, their luggage was in a car accompanying them. We all shared the same room. In Shaliwahan, I had the darshan of a Naga Sadhu (Saint) sitting under a shade of a banyan tree. He was six and a half feet tall, well built, with big reddish eyes, long hair, and deadlocks, with ash smeared on his body.

I tried to approach him, but it was challenging to connect. When I bowed down to pay my respect in the evening, he asked me why I hesitated to ask and clarify my doubts. He told me to meet him after dinner. Accordingly, I bowed down and sat for a satsang. In simple language, he explained that the human body combines five elements - earth, water, fire, air, and space. It is the property of the universe, and we are the custodians during this life. At the end of our life, the body turns into ash. Ash symbolises purity and reality, showing that the body and ash are the same, only time differs. When a Saint smears ash, it reminds them of the truth that he is the Atma (Consciousness). He has to burn away anava (the ego, sense of I and mine) by acquiring the right knowledge in this life. Being in this constant awareness of the truth, the Sadhu remains absorbed continuously in pursuit of a higher goal in life. Ethics, love, compassion, and calmness become their natural habit in all situations. Similarly, people apply vibuthi in the middle of the eyebrows for a unique vibration and a reminder of the Divine truth.

I asked him how an individual can realise their real purpose in life. He explained that our world reflects our habits, intellect, mind, and heart. Our senses perceive them, which may be different from reality. Our happiness or unhappiness is due to the expectations of the world. We either worry about the past or imagine the future and invite sadness, stress, and frustration. Enthusiasm comes when we concentrate on the present as it moves our energy towards actions. Awareness moves you to take the right action or inaction. Amidst your ethical actions, consciousness (Atma) continues to help you move forward. On further enquiry, he laid down the road map to realise your purpose. Few of the important points:

1. Draw a map to focus your energy on it.
2. Be grateful to everyone who has shown love and compassion, and pardon all those who have caused harm.
3. Be constantly aware of your intellect, mind, emotions, and body.
4. Invest 100% energy in your purpose rather than spending excessive time thinking about the future or analysing the past.
5. Having done your best, avoid getting attached to the results thereof.

I asked Naga Sadhu to explain what actions I could take during parikrama to attain a higher level of awareness. He said that dissatisfaction, unhappiness and discontent sets in the absence of fullness. Cheerfulness, peace and sleep get disturbed. To remain happy, always repeat a mantra during parikrama. When continuously repeated, a mantra having high vibrating energy protects you. It clears your mind from worries about the future or past regrets. The clarity removes your blockages and moves you to a blissful state. Give your hundred per cent in thoughts, actions, and speech in spiritual practices. Energy generated by this combination will raise your efforts to a higher level, and you will attain fullness, peace, and happiness. Certain things are beyond you, so the results of your action should not bind you. You commit and give a hundred per cent of your effort and be indifferent to outcomes. In the absence of regrets, fear, or anxiety - the mind turns within, the individual remains peaceful and cheerful, knowledge widens, and consciousness guides them to success. In short, he said that it was the key to attain blissfulness. I decided to follow his simple but powerful technique, to keep myself occupied with mantras during parikrama and enjoy the present.

The next morning while going for a bath in Narmada Mai, three puppies escorted me to the Ghat. Along the way, they pulled my dhoti and blocked my way when I took the wrong path. Similar instances also happened at other places during the parikrama. Dogs escorted me for miles and returned from a certain point. Initially, I was afraid of dogs, but I realised that as a Divine help, they keep me safe and on track. After the bath at Narmada Mai, I went to the Shiva Temple. After having the darshan of Lord Shiva, I met the Temple priest, Mr Madan Lal Dubey. He comes every morning and evening, cleans the Temple premises and does puja and aarti. He told me that Shaliwahan was the capital of Hindu King Shaliwahan, a legendary emperor of India and the founder of the Hindu Saka Calendar.

After balbhog (breakfast), I started for Shahastra Dhara, Balgoan. The area was very fertile. Sugarcane, banana, wheat, bajara, and vegetables are grown. People seemed to have a comfortable life. At Balgoan, I had the darshan at Buteshwar Shiva Mandir. The complex has a vast gowshala that shelters around five hundred old cows left by people when they stop giving milk.

Similarly, people generally do not care for individuals in this materialistic world after their utility is over, even if they have served them for years. Generally, it is true for society, organisations, families, and relatives. However, few enlightened people do take care with love and compassion for the non-useful animals amid worldly chaos. I inquired from a Saint about the relevance of gowshala. In Sanatana Dharma (Hindu Religion), he said the cow is considered a universal Mother and narrated a very inspiring story.

Sindhutai, a tribal child from Wardha district having passed the 4th class, was married at the age of ten to a thirty-year-old man. She faced many problems post-marriage and fought with the forest department and landlords against exploiting local tribal women. Sindhutai had three sons, and at the age of twenty, during the ninth month's pregnancy, her husband thrashed her badly until the unconscious state. Her husband thought that she was dead. He threw her into a cowshed to make it appear that the animal had wounded her to death. As she remained unconscious, a cow stood over her and protected her against all the animals. When she regained consciousness, she gave birth to a baby girl, Mamta, under the cow's protection. As you have protected me during my distress, she promised the cow I would protect others in their time of trouble. Under desperation, she went to her mother's place, who refused shelter. At that time, providing refuge to a married daughter was considered wrong by the tribe. She used to beg for a living. To protect herself from men, she often spent nights at cemeteries. Finally, being fed up with her miserable life, she decided to commit suicide. When she lay down on the railway tracks with her daughter to commit suicide, she heard a man crying for food and water. She remembered her promise made to the cow. She set aside her thought of suicide, started begging, and gave food and water to the crying man. The older man came to her in the form of God. He told her that she had some higher purpose in life. She needs to contribute a lot to this world.

She wondered how she could contribute to the world as she had nothing and no one to help. One day she was sitting under a tree with her child. A woodcutter had violently cut the tree branch, which was still hanging by one string, giving shelter to both. A spark of light flashed that if a half-chopped tree branch can provide protection, I can also do something for this world.

Sindhutai, in her life, had seen many children abandoned by their parents. An idea came to her that she could adopt them as her own. Over a period, over 1,050 orphaned children have been nurtured in her Ashram in Pune. Many of the children whom she adopted are well-educated lawyers and doctors. At the age of 80, her husband regretfully came back to her. She accepted him as her child. She has received over 273 international and national awards for her dedication and work. She uses the award money to buy land and make a home for her children. She has an unlimited source of energy and compelling inspiration. The story shows the power and usefulness of the mother cow. Hearing the story, I prayed to Narmada Mai to shower similar powerful inspiration.

As I walked towards Khal Ghat, an elderly gentleman wearing a dhoti and kurta (Indian dress) with vibuthi (sandal paste) on his forehead greeted me. I responded, saying, Narmade Har. After talking to him, I learned he had completed Narmada Parikrama five times. He was curious about my residence and where I started my parikrama. He asked me – "are you doing the parikrama alone?" I remembered Sindhutai and the cow's story and replied - though you see me walking alone, Narmada Mai is with me. He was soft-spoken, however, an enlightened and pious soul. We sat under a tree, and after drinking water from the hand pump, we shared a biscuit packet and started talking about many things, including his experience and work. He leads a brahmacharya life, is associated with enlightened Saints, and travels to spiritual centres across India.

I asked him how an individual gets attached or detached from the world's mundane aspects. He said – "You can look at this world from many perspectives, depending upon the external stimuli, the perception, observations and options transmitted to the intelligence. Depending upon the level and refinement of the intellect, it decides on the action. It returns its decision to the mind, which is further conveyed to the sense organs to take action.

In today's materialistic world, we look through the lens of intelligence, mind, ego, or a combination thereof. Mind is a storehouse of memories, and the ego is of an individual's I-ness. Based on limited knowledge, we believe what is logical. We create bonding with the universe, objects, and situations. It gives a feeling of scarcity and a sense of nonfulfillment.

On getting deep-rooted in the spiritual path, we view the world as connected, an extension of our Atma (consciousness), and a pure manifestation of God. Aligning ourselves with compassion, elevating our intelligence with spirituality, shredding our memory and ego, and surrendering ourselves to the Divine is essential for building a relationship with the supreme and self. It helps us act ethically, bringing love, peace, and forgiveness. We accept everything as they are with purity and sacredness; in turn, it kindles the highest form of energy within us – "love."

Attachment is essential for having a meaning for an individual to put effort into the object thereof. Without passion, life or relationship is unsustainable. A mother feeds her child, sometimes sacrificing her food out of affection towards her child. Excellence in any field occurs through effort and sacrifice created by extraordinary attachment to the subject. If one is not attached, engagement does not happen, and boredom sets. An individual spends more effort and time on the area of their liking. Getting hooked on worldly objects or relationships in this physical world is effortless due to limited time, effort, and results. An earthly relationship is limited, based on the individual's priority, shifting nature which is devoid of lasting fulfilment. As the situation dives, one does not find satisfaction in the relationship, boredom sets in, and happiness turns into misery. Hence, undertake worldly actions as a duty without getting attached to it.

We waste our time on useless gossip, arguments, and negative stories which get stored in our minds. We attach value to others' feelings and opinions, and eventually, others' opinion becomes the catalyst to destroy our strength and knowledge.

"Birds of the same feather flock together" is a popular phrase. In a group, people influence each other. In the process, the power of discrimination decreases, leading to self-ignorance, and all sorts of fear and doubt set in, creating imaginary problems leading to conflict within and outside. By design, human nature tends to reflect on a single wrong experience repeatedly, leading to hatred and boredom, which disturbs the balance of the body and leads to mental and physical diseases.

The result is impure when two things like water and oil do not bond. A genuine and bonding relationship happens in how water and milk mix effortlessly. With a feeling of belongingness with everyone, separation disappears, unity with the Divine, and creation starts. There are two types of energy power - animal and human. Animal energy is aggressive, limited, a one-sided mechanical force, filled with anger and lacking intelligence. Human energy is alive, awakened, and filled with love and discrimination. Children derive strength from their purity. Even though younger, children are the master of the house since they attract everyone's attention and ensure they get what they want done.

Attachment to the Divine energy creates self-awareness, which dissolves impurities of the mind and body. Similarly, devotion through satsang (the company of good people for communion with the truth), sadhana (daily spiritual practice), and sewa (service) have tremendous power. It reduces dependence on the world, restlessness, and discontent, unveils Maya and creates lasting happiness. It is essential to understand that a person needs to focus on their effort rather than the results for eternal happiness.

My younger daughter Meenakshi Mishra had designed a beautiful artefact. I wanted her to preserve the same, and she was determined to dispose it off. She told me that we had to tear apart our exemplary work after the examination and feedback session at the School of Design. If you possess your art, a sense of false achievement sets in, and you will never grow beyond it. For improvement, one must give up their work, however good it may be. This way, the mind gets energised and feels the urge to do better the next time, which is creativity. I was able to connect the teachings with the example given by my daughter.

I asked him – how can we change our habits and behaviour to attain blissfulness? He gave a simple solution. Believe that everything is a play scripted by the Supreme Divine and perform your role as per the script. With devotion and spiritual practices come purity, animal instinct decreases, and human energy rises within the self. It is, therefore, essential to have an attachment with God for an everlasting relationship. Enhance your effort to be in union with the Divine. Be aware of your thoughts, ensure ethical action, forgive yourself and others, and show gratefulness for love and care. After a while, your thoughts will start reflecting inwards. Follow your inner voice, and discriminate between right and wrong. Thus, dependence on the world for happiness will decrease, and the higher consciousness will take over; permanent joy and bliss will be the new way of life.

I tried to grasp the teachings while walking from

Khal Ghat to Balaji Sankatmochan Hanuman Mandir. I wanted the wisdom to soak in and started considering different perspectives and realities. Therefore, I decided to spend a night at the Mandir beside the bridge on a hilltop. After meditation, puja and aarti, I had dinner and slept. The next morning - feeling energised, I started for Chinchili. The passage onward was dusty, hilly and scary. I entered a different world with ravines, pagdandi (narrow lanes), and thorny bushes with sides raised by natural mud walls. The area did not have direction signs at crossroads, and walking through it gave a ghostly experience. Not a single soul was in sight, and one mistake could lead to the wrong direction for a few kilometres. The ravines pushed me to practice what I had learned from the Saint. I prayed to God for help, developed courage, and followed my intuition in the absence of any signs. Majority of the time, I found myself on the right track. A lesson for me to contemplate within, and the answer was available.

At Chinchili, I had lunch at the residence of Mr Hari OM. He was a poor, unemployed person having three daughters and a son. He wore torn trousers; his house looked depleted with the roof thatched with cardboard/hay, walls and mud flooring, which needed immediate repairs. Still, the family sacrificed their essential need to provide food and tea to all parikramawasis. Hari OM is a living example of how trust and belief in the Divine brings fulfilment, commitment, connection, compassion, and patience, even without worldly wealth. I tried giving him money to buy biscuits for their children; however, he refused and, with a smile, said, I have to go a long way and will require it.

After lunch, I came to Narmade Har Baba Ashram.

After an afternoon rest, I managed through dusty village roads and mud ravines to Ram Mandir and Sukleshwar Mahadev Mandir, Brahman Gaon. An older woman living alone takes care of the Mandir. She is a widow with seven kids having a meagre income. It was freezing, and I had to spend the night on the veranda of the Mandir overlooking Narmada Mai. I asked the caretaker, "How do you manage to serve when you have shortages of necessary worldly comfort? She said - Mai (Narmada) takes care. We are just a madhayam (instrument). So amidst all the hue and cry, you find examples of two families deprived of basic worldly needs, serving others. They remain fulfilled, happy, and blissful because of their union with the Divine Power in the lap of Narmada Mai.

While I was walking, some comfortable and awkward flashbacks came in a continuum as a movie. I was a relatively intelligent individual but was an average student. I wrote my graduation examination amidst violent and mass strikes and boycotts by agitating students. Then I did not fear for my life, knowing that my life was in danger, but today I fear tomorrow. I did exceptionally well in my career with many landmarks; however, I could not pay the mortgage of my house and just managed to save it from bank attachment due to more than expected income from one major consulting assignment in a startup company. Known for my social skills and friends circle, today, my situation is, as described by Taylor Coleridge - "water, water, everywhere, not a drop to drink." I had robust health but faced the worst health crisis with life-threatening diseases. As a dedicated spiritual practitioner, I still seek spiritual guidance. In short, life has been a roller coaster; however, I have enjoyed and learned every moment.

From Brahman Gaon, I started for Mohipura. To my surprise, the land in this patch was very fertile. Farmers grew cotton, wheat, banana, sugarcane, and vegetables. At Nalbai is the Sangam of rivers Deb and Narmada Mai. The water in River Deb was knee-deep but sparkling. From Nalbai to Lahora, it was mostly barren and rocky. Lahora is the tapobhumi (place of tapasya/austerity) of Kapil Muni, the founder of Sankhya Yoga. The road to Narmada and Shiva Temple, Lahora, was well decorated with banners of Sanskrit shlokas. An old Haveli adjacent to the Temple, having ancient architecture with long wooden pillars, thatched rooftop, and mud flooring, is the dedicated place for parikramawasis. Cooking happens on wood fires, and utensils have an antique look. All parikramawasis get proper food.

While bhakts were preparing food, parikramawasis and Saints started discussing the importance of nutrition in life. The quality and quantity of food determine our thoughts and behaviour. Therefore, awareness of what we consume is important in our life. On reflection, I correlated that my wife Neeru Mishra, a practising yoga teacher, also spends a lot of time explaining the importance of having sattvic (sentient) food since it is conducive to physical, mental, and emotional well-being. It enhances calmness and balances the equilibrium within. Rajasic (mutative) food acts as a stimulant, increasing energy and arousing agitation, passion, and emotion. Tamasic (static) food due to impurity is harmful, decreases the power within, brings dullness, and is responsible for stress.

After the discussion, we all had food and slept for some time. It was a pleasant and peaceful experience being in Lahora. I came to Mohipura in the evening and stayed at Maa Rewa Ashram, Samadhi of Swami Amritanand Puri. On the occasion of Republic Day, a village cricket league was in full swing with prize money of twenty-five thousand, ten thousand, and five thousand rupees for the champion, runner and third-position teams, respectively. In the evening, villagers gathered at the Ashram to finalise the program for Republic Day. On the occasion of Republic Day, everyone went to attend a flag-hoisting ceremony. I offered to teach yoga to a special child.

After finishing the yoga class, I came to Ram Mandir, Pipluud. There were a few more parikramawasis staying in the Mandir. After meditation, puja and aarti, we all went for dinner, where twenty members of a joint family stayed under one roof. Their house was in a huge complex with all modern amenities. The place's attraction was a large, decorated swing with brass ornamented ropes on the veranda. All the members had responsibilities allotted, and they managed them very smoothly. It was a pleasant experience to see the working of a joint family. We had an excellent dinner in a traditional style, with chapattis, five vegetables, curd, and sweets. Everyone was worried that they must abandon the house once the dam becomes operational, as one hundred ninety-six other villages, including Pipluud, would be submerged in the Narmada. The next day I taught yoga to homemakers suffering from thyroid, back pain and diabetes. Our yoga practice lasted for two and a half hours. All the participants promised to continue yoga.

Around 10.00 am, I left Pipluud and came to Swami Shri Satyanand Maharaj Ashram, Kasaravad, through the lush green fertile land. I met three Saints Moni Baba, Tyagi Baba, and Aghori Baba (Naga Sadhu). Moni Baba observed silence from sunrise to sunset and was in seven years parikrama phase. During the day, Tyagi and Moni Baba made garlands from Tulsi beads. Aghori Baba, 6 feet 4 inches tall, had a well-built body and, from his talk, seemed to be a learned Saint. I took the opportunity to spend time with him and understand the nature of energy alignment and its relation to health and spirituality. He said the entire creation, from the universe to the smallest particle, is an energy centre. Every atom is and has energy. The Sun, planets, earth, water, fire, air, and space are energy. The union of energy gives us food, shelter, river, ocean, and rain. We get energised after food; when we excrete, it returns to the soil. The cycle continues as the Sun's heat evaporates water from the ocean and falls as rainwater, fills the river/sea. The body, comprised of the five elements, returns to the atmosphere after death.

The world is one energy centre with a fixed amount of land, air, water, and other circulating elements. It cannot add anything more, not even a small seed. Matter and energy are inter-convertible. They change forms without destruction or re-creation. Everything in this world has a cycle of destruction and rebirth. It is essential to build and conserve energy because energy is finite.

Humans exist in a sthula sarira (physical body) and a sushma sarira (subtle body). The physical body includes the biological mass. The subtle body is energy that moves through energy channels (nadi) connected by nodes of psychic energy called chakra. The seven main chakras (energy centres) are arranged vertically along the axial channel (Sushumna nadi) in the spinal cord in our body. Eighty-eight thousand subtle nerves connect the seven centres. Individual chakras have different colours, mantra (bija), subtle elements (tantra) and shapes. As per yogic philosophy, chanting and meditation on the chakras enhance radiant inner energy (prana) from the lowest to the highest chakra to balance mind-body coordination. The efficiency of a human being means converting optimum energy through the charkas and blending the appropriate power with the environment to fulfil their purpose.

Muladhara (Root) Chakra represents the Earth element and is at the spinal cord's base. This chakra's Kundalini (the feminine energy) is either dormant or active. From Muladhara Chakra, energy rises to higher Chakras. The second energy centre representing the Water element is the Swadhisthan (Sacral) Chakra, situated behind the sex organ. Her energy is expressed either as lust or creativity. The third energy centre representing the Fire element is around the navel called Manipur (Solar Plexus). Manipur Chakra is associated with greed, jealousy, happiness, or generosity. The fourth energy centre representing the Air element is behind the Anahata (Heart) Chakra. It generates love, confidence, hatred, and fear. The fifth energy centre representing the Space element is around the throat region known as Vishudhi (Throat) Chakra. It expresses gratitude, grief, relationship, conflict, or misery. The sixth energy centre between eyebrows, Agya (Guru /Third Eye) Chakra, expresses awareness, knowledge, and anger. Finally, at the top of the head lies the seventh energy centre known as the Sahasrara (Crown) Chakra. It is the purest and highest centre where pure consciousness resides. When energy travels to the seventh chakra, the feminine Kundalini power unites with the masculine Shiva Shakti, invoking self-realisation full of bliss.

I further enquired about how to live a healthy life.

He replied that under pressure, disturbance and negativity, energy gets blocked on appropriate chakra forming knots and obstructing the natural flow of energy from Muladhara to Sahasrara chakra. Blockages in the chakras lead us to lust, greed, jealousy, hatred, fear, grief, misery, conflict, and anger. With impurities in the energy centres, individuals still sweat it out by working extremely hard to sustain life. It is at the cost of high or low blood pressure, ulcers, anger, jealousy, and other undesired results.

As we raise awareness, we observe sensations in different body parts depending on our perception, thoughts, feelings, emotion, or excitement. When angry, the area between the eyebrows ignites. When unhappy or while expressing gratitude throat starts to choke. Likewise, when an individual is sad, there is a feeling in the throat, and when they want to express gratitude, they cannot describe it in words, and we often say that the throat chokes. The heart centre senses emotions such as hatred, jealousy or love. An individual can observe the blockages and free energy if attention is on the chakras. Chanting and meditation on the chakras are powerful ways to dissolve negative energy. Over time, energy balances around the five elements, impurities disappear, and positive qualities blossom, leading to a healthy life.

I asked Aghori Baba how we could achieve bliss. He said that we remain unaware, act with limited knowledge, commit mistakes, and defend ourselves due to our negative dispositions. We gradually move down the winding lane, leading to misery and unacceptable or unethical behaviour. We must spend priority time at satsang, sadhana, sewa and meditation. Spending time in solitary life helps us overcome negativity and convert ourselves into creative, happy, generous, loving, confident, grateful, knowledgeable, and blissful beings. I was thankful to Aghori Baba for explaining the path to purify the impurities for leading a blissful life. I felt blessed to be in his company.

Along with other parikramawasis, I went to Narmada Mai for an evening bath. After the puja, we sat for the satsang, chanting mantras and singing bhajans. Aghori Baba narrated a lot of Sanskrit shlokas and their meaning. Moni Baba sang bhajans in praise of Lord Krishna. Except for Aghori Baba, we slept in a hall. The night temperature was freezing. The next morning, we had a hot water bath. After the bath and morning rituals, we all proceeded to Raj Ghat. One face, Dutta Mandir, established in 1992 by Tembo Swami on the bank of Narmada Mai, is the centre of devotion and attraction at Raj Ghat. People in their traditional dress had come to Dutta Mandir, and the atmosphere at Raj Ghat was full of delight. From Raj Ghat onwards is Shoolpani Jhari (Jungle).

Walking through the green and rocky terrain had its wonder, hardship, and fulfilment. By now, I had started enjoying being within myself. I hardly bothered about the outside world or what others thought of me. Though the terrain was tough, I realised that by being inward, I became a storehouse of enthusiasm and strength and uncovered my mental and physical potential. The beautiful scenery, the wonders, and the expanse of Narmada Mai gave me a lot of happiness and peace. At times due to the freezing weather, I had sleepless nights. However, the morning dip in Narmada Mai was refreshing and energising. Hardships and inwardness only enhanced my endurance. Over time, I got used to the new way of living and started loving it.

OM Peace, Peace, Peace
Narmade Har.

Immersion

During an environmental trek, students got an opportunity to see a butterfly cocoon struggling to come out. One of the students caught a few butterflies and, along with them, carried the butterfly cocoon back for an experiment. With a pair of scissors, he snipped off the remaining bit of the cocoon to end the suffering of the butterfly. The butterfly then emerged quickly out of the cocoon with shrivelled wings. Unable to fly, the butterfly kept crawling around with tiny wings and a swollen body, whereas other butterflies were flying. The student got puzzled and asked his teacher why the butterfly could not fly. The teacher explained that restricting the cocoon and the struggle needed by the butterfly to get itself through the small opening is God's way of forcing fluid from the butterfly's body into its wings. It prepares the insect for flying once it is out of the cocoon. Later, she narrated the incident in class and drew parallels with life. It is essential to face struggles and tackle challenges in life. It is a mechanism to help individuals develop their thinking and physical power for success.

Shoolpani (name of Lord Shiva) ki Jhari (jungle) is an important location in the parikrama. The entire area is surrounded by hills, jungles and inhabited by tribes. At Raj Ghat, people advised me to avoid going through Shoolpani ki Jhari (jungle) as the path has a high possibility of accidents due to steep gradients, uneven roads, and dangerous mountain terrain. There is always a fear of being ransacked by local tribes. I, however, decided to venture through Shoolpani Jungle. The road to Bhik Khera was very dusty. After that, a tar road with steep gradients passes through Pendra, Pitori, Bhamta, Pallia, Bhaunti, Vijasean, Morkatta, and Borgkheri. At around 6.00 pm, I reached Pallia. I was exhausted and unable to locate a place for a night stay. A school-going girl met me on the road. On learning that I had failed to find a proper place for rest, she told me that I could rest in the Mandir. She went out of her way to escort me for half a kilometre to Nardeshwar Mandir, which had accommodation for parikramawasis.

Saint Bharav Das welcomed me at the Mandir, took good care and prepared dinner for himself and others in the Temple. After the evening meditation, puja, and aarti, we sang a few bhajans, followed by a spiritual discourse on Bhog (offering food to the Divine). Why do we offer food to the Divine before eating? The Saint said we learn from books that the knowledge enters our mind after learning, although the writing in the book remains. Thus, the knowledge is transformed from gross (text) to subtle form (mind). Similarly, when we offer food to the Divine in a gross form, he accepts it subtly and offers his blessings to the food (subtle form), which becomes prasad (blessed food). Prasad nourishes our bodies and helps us remain healthy and balanced.

After the discourse, all the villagers left, and after dinner, we slept. The next day I got up at 3.30 am. After bath and morning rituals, I started for Borgkheri along the tar road. The route had steep gradients. En route, I ate two packets of biscuits given by a bhakt at Vijasean for lunch. Around 4.00 pm, I reached Mr Hiralal's (ex-sarpanch) house in Borgkheri. I decided to spend the night at his place since the tar road ends at this village, and after that, one has to walk through pagdandi (footway) and jungle roads. Along the route were a few colonies with a sparing population at three/four kilometres intervals. Parikramawasi usually distributes toffee/biscuits to kids after exchanging Narmade Har. In a few places, kids also asked for money. Watching young kids climbing up and down the mountain to receive biscuits and toffees distributed by parikramawasis was fascinating.

Hiralal's house had four rooms, a kitchen, a washing area, and a shop in front, and by its side was a small open area with mud flooring covered with a tin shed. It was the resting place for parikramawasi. Construction is going on to raise the height of the Narmada Dam. Along with neighbouring villages, Borgkheri will submerge into Narmada Mai soon. Village residents were shifted to different places, so houses in the village were dilapidated. Villagers had received compensation for their land. Money received as compensation in place of land and house is spent on liquor and other non-essential desires, which is disturbing. For example, many people had purchased a motorcycle on loan out of compensation money though they did not have enough to live a decent life.

In the evening, Hiralal's shop became a lively place. Villagers gathered around the shop to spend leisure time and buy their daily requirements. By 7.00 pm, they left the shop and went to their residences. After dinner, we talked about the jungle, the activities of people, and the new colonies. Mr Hiralal warned me to distribute toffee or biscuits only to kids along the way and not to give them any money even if they insist. Due to the extreme cold and wind at night, I was unable to sleep comfortably. In the morning, I had the darshan of Narmada Mai from Hiralal's house.

From Borgkheri to Kula, I had to walk on muddy/loose pebbles road with steep slopes at times of 60/70 degree gradient. The area had an Adivasi population. At Kula, I met a Saint who narrated an exciting story. A Scientist came to a Saint intending to attain self-knowledge. After the initial talk, the Saint offered tea to the Scientist. While pouring, tea started overflowing from the cup to the saucer. The Scientist brought this to the notice of the Saint. The Saint replied that if the mind is ignorant, spirituality will spill outside instead of being absorbed. Our mind gets filled with knowledge received by sensory organs during interaction with worldly matters. Corresponding thoughts and actions move our attention to the outer world. Like a cloud in the sky overshadows the Sun, so does ignorance overpower the mind. Therefore, it is essential to empty the mind as spiritual awareness begins in emptiness.

The collage of nature has plants of many shades with sprinkles of weeds surrounding them. To have a good crop, we need to plant and nurture appropriate seeds by sowing them in the right season, providing adequate manure and water, and preventing destruction by taking the right actions. Seeds that are important to human beings for lasting happiness are love, peace, and bliss. Nurturing them is possible by trending on the steps of the spiritual path. It is essential to choose a quiet place where an individual can sit comfortably and immerse in their heart and mind. The mind will wander in many directions; however, with dhyana (meditation), the mind can concentrate in one order for a few minutes before walking in other directions. In the transition between the movements, the individual gets a glimpse of blissfulness. As the process continues, an individual becomes accustomed to new feelings. They can also meditate on an object or a leaf for some time. While doing this, they can overcome their worries. With regular meditation, waves in the mind become still, and seeds of blissfulness start mushrooming.

He further elaborated that individuals should be aware of their thoughts, discriminate between right and wrong, and commit to action only on the right and ethical issues. Individuals must believe in themselves, walk a virtuous path, and stop worrying. An individual is responsible for sowing and nurturing the right seeds in the collage of their world. It is futile to attach value to others' opinions and spend time in useless talk and unnecessary gossip. It only adds a layer of ignorance. Instead, weed out seeds of ignorance by investing energy in sewa, sadhana, satsang, and sadvichar (virtues). Atma is all-pervading, all-powerful and all-knowing. Mantras and rituals help erase the noise of Maya and enter the domain of knowledge. The meditation experience soaks an individual to contentment in waking, sleeping, and dreaming states. It clears useless and limited thoughts and emotions of ignorance. For self-realisation, an individual must be absorbed in self and experience peace and happiness. It will make an individual cheerful, filled with energy and allow the heart and mind to melt as they enter into themselves. I felt blessed as it gave me steps to move up the ladder of happiness and knowledge. I learned different meditation techniques, which I could practice during my parikrama.

After the discourse, I quietly sat for an hour, trying to absorb the message. Then, I started for Gonsha, tapobhumi of August Muni. Due to rocky and non-fertile soil, dependence on agriculture is limited. Fishing is a substantial source of diet and income in the area. Despite crocodiles in the river, local people use small boats to cross and venture into the river for fishing. Lakhangiri Maharaj, during his parikrama, was looted by tribal with only a loincloth left on him. After the incident, Narmada Mai blessed Maharaj and instructed him to work amongst the tribal for their upliftment. As a result, the Maharaj stayed back and established Maa Narmada Dutt Ashram (also known as Lakhangiri Maharaj Ashram) on the bank of Narmada Mai in Ghonsa village.

Lakhangiri Maharaj sowed the seed for ensuring the well-being and self-development of the tribes of the Shoolpani Jungle. The Maharaj developed a great rapport with tribal groups and wholeheartedly worked for their material and spiritual upliftment by providing education, farming, necessary amenities, spiritual discourses, and ethical practices. His mission was to create happiness and fulfilment among the tribes. He collected and distributed clothes, seeds of cereals, and useful plants from various sources in pursuance thereof. Through his effort, the local population got educated, uplifted, and after that, they stopped looting parikramawasis. Maa Narmada Dutt Ashram was a pleasant place where Narmada Mai flows between the steep slopes of the Vindhya and Satpura ranges of mountains. The sight of crocodiles enjoying sunbathing on a dune at the river bank enhances the site's beauty.

After my prayer and meditation, I went to have a darshan of an elderly Saint from Uttarakhand staying in the

Ashram. He had an extremely positive aura. A few other Saints were also in attendance. He gave a sermon on life's essence in a very soft and smiling tone. At birth, we weigh three or four kilograms. Milk and food intake support the child in his growth. Whatever we eat or drink gets converted into our body and mind. The quality and quantity of the food we consume determine our thoughts and behaviour. Self-awareness and knowledge require concentration, focus, alertness, and silence. We can realise our true nature to the extent that we raise our energy and vitality. Eating more makes us sleepy since energy is required to digest the food. Under the circumstances, the energy needed for self-knowledge is unavailable. Therefore, eating only sattvic food and in a limited quantity is essential. Balance and alignment of intellect, mind, ego, and emotions are prerequisites for an awakened and vibrant state. Spiritual knowledge comes from the Divine and ignorance, the cause of all our miseries, arises from Maya.

Jealousy, anger and hatred are due to ego, lust and ignorance, whereas knowledge carries love, compassion, and care. Fullness is possible when an individual stays inward, peaceful, confident, present, and concentrated. Uplifting ideas come when an individual surrenders to the Divine. With continued practice over some time, the state of awakened consciousness becomes the new reality.

In awakened consciousness, one finds no difference in worldly happiness and misery, gain or loss. With renewed confidence and surrender, an individual can effortlessly swim against the tide of Maya. When one submits self to God and puts full effort into the right actions, the energy of the Divine and self merge. That energy of higher order completes the entire task effortlessly without attachment, and the fruit of action, good or bad, will not be binding. As an observer, enjoy the drama of this world and act as a witness.

With positive inspiration, I started my journey around noon for Khemlet. The pagdandi route is through hillocks for about a kilometre along the Narmada. Then I had to suddenly climb and descend for five hundred to thousand feet with steep gradients accompanied by the harrowing sound of the wind. I missed the right path and had to return after walking a distance of two kilometres through two hills. The point where I missed the road, the view of Narmada Mai, was blissful. She comes from the north, turns west, and again turns north after flowing for two kilometres, in between the turns; Maa Narmada Dutt Ashram stands tall. The hills made the journey difficult as well as meaningful. Nevertheless, I could cover a distance of six kilometres in four hours.

From Khemlet to Shemlet, the route is through a dry river bed. At one point, I missed the right crossing and took the wrong nala (path through the river bed) into a dense forest. A lady with her son accompanied me to the right way. She provided a lunch of bajara (maze) ki roti and dal. After lunch, she asked her sons to help me climb a steep hill with slippery loose pebbles and mud. In Shemlet, I spent a night at the house of the village Sarpanch, Mr Gulab Singh. People in Shoolpani are very cooperative and went out of their way to help me. Mr Gulab Singh was an accommodating man who tried to put effort into village development. Officials and affluent politicians had visited Shemlet a week back and promised the villagers to resolve their basic issues. He had been to the District Headquarters to resolve village issues; however, he was unable to resolve any of them due to the apathy of officials. In the evening, people came to meet him with their problems. After dinner, I went to sleep. Early morning after meditation, bath and aarti, I continued my journey.

Narmada Mai and mantra chanting have kept the valley vibrant and positive. The micro-individual and the macro-universe have integrated to make one's life inspiring and useful. "Paraspar Devo Bhava" (serving humankind is serving God) and "You have a right over your action, not the results thereof" are practised in the valley. We need to learn from the action of people living in the valley. During the day, I pondered the usual notorious intentional-behaviour gap, a few incidents and the learning from the parikrama. As a movie, thoughts started flashing vividly in front of my eyes. An individual has a body, and within, the creator resides. People and situations create temptations in life – be aware and move away from them, fulfil your basic needs through ethical means, and accept nothing for collection. Otherwise, opposite energies will work in a tangent direction and hijack the real purpose of existence.

In the world, opposites coexist, such as day and night, cruelty and innocence, benevolence and deception. People get disturbed when they spend time only on achieving worldly desires. The brain becomes restless and the body sleepless. Hardships, adverse situations, and an attitude of apprehension are standard features during the initial days of the spiritual journey. Accept such conditions and avoid confrontation. When under stress, relax under a neem tree, and calmness prevails. As individuals rise to higher levels, ordinary things do not allure them. Experience and a consistent relationship with God help one remain brave and tranquil. It enhances physical and mental endurance.

On the way to Bhadal (MP), I had to climb steep hills with loose pebbles. I lost my balance in a few places and fell twice. However, the prevailing thoughts gave me the courage to return and continue my parikrama. On my way from Bhadal (MP) to Bhadal (Maharashtra), the hilly road had steep gradients. After crossing the village Bhadal (MP), I lost my way and took a pagdandi which led to the mountaintop overseeing the Jarkan River. The slope had a gradient of ninety degrees, forming a rock wall. The sight was frightening, and in no way could I climb down. Not a single soul was in sight. I roamed from 1.00 pm to 3.00 pm, looking for the right road to climb down the hill. Suddenly a man approached and told me I was moving in the wrong direction. He accompanied me to the right path and suddenly, after that, disappeared. I tried looking for him but was unable to locate him.

After drinking water, I descended the path through rocky stairs and slopes to reach River Jarkan. With high concentration, focus, and balance, I could come down. On crossing the river, I again lost the path. A little boy accompanied me to the house of Mr Kalu Ram, a merchant with four donkeys, four horses, and twenty cattle. He had a shop in the front room of his house; next to it was a temporary shed covered with cardboard for parikramawasi, and attached to it was a space for his animals. Mr Kalu and I had dinner, and after that, he started seeing a movie on his mobile. I had a sound sleep under the temporary shed. The next morning, for a bath, I went to the well, located around five hundred feet below his house.

En route on my journey to Bhawari, two other Parikramawasi joined me. One of them, Mr Aravind (name changed), hailed from West Bengal and had started his parikrama from Amarkantak. He was a healthy, built individual who wanted to commit suicide and left his house due to family feuds. By luck, he ended up in Amarkantak and met a Saint. He started living in his Ashram. After six months, he took to Narmada Parikrama, and his mental disposition changed.

After covering a distance of around ten kilometres from Bhadal, we were tired. Therefore, we stopped at the house of an old lady for rest. She prepared lunch for us as we rested underneath the raised platform to store hays. After meditation and lunch, we proceeded to Khaparmal. The steepest climb so far was between Bhawari and Khaparmal. With the help of Mr Aravind, it took me about an hour to climb a distance of around a thousand feet. Narmada Mai sends much-needed support at the appropriate time.

Around 4.00 pm, while crossing Khaparmal, we were stopped by Mr Mantio. He requested us to spend the night at his place. He told us that it was impossible to cover a distance of four kilometres before sunset due to the hilly terrain. The slope ahead was very steep, with many loose pebbles, stones, and loose mud. Mr Mantio has a small farm and works in Gujarat as a labourer. At his request, we stayed in his under-construction house with a stack of bricks, two cots (one for Mantio and another for his mother), a machan (loft), and a swing tied to two pillars for the child. After a delicious dinner prepared by the family, we slept in one corner of the room with other occupants - Mantio, his mom, wife, five girl children, hens, chicks, cats, calf, dog, and two puppies.

In the morning, the family was having fun chatting, laughing, and consuming tea around the fire in the room. At 8.00 am, they all went to fetch water from one and a half kilometres uphill. As we stepped out, we had a panoramic darshan of Narmada Mai from the house. We started for Bhawana around 8.00 am without freshening up due to water shortage and seeing the family's difficulty fetching the same. The patch forward was very uneven, with slippery pebbles and loose stones. It was scary climbing down due to the steep descent and unstable path. Finally, around 9.00 am, we came across a spring and took this opportunity to freshen up. After the bath, we did our puja and aarti and, by 12.30 pm, reached Bhawana, covering a distance of eight kilometres.

In the jungle, the elevation and slope of hills and the gushing sound of winds became my world. Along the path, the gradients were sharp with loose stones. Steep rocky ridge made the journey dangerous, and a small error was enough to cost a life. With intense focus, I moved slowly, being aware of every movement of my body, deliberate of each foot placement. I ensured to handgrip every protruding stone or branch of a tree. With precision, as I moved forward, calmness prevailed within. Sense perceptions increased, and things started looking sharper and more colourful. I felt in tune with life. The bliss of mindfulness, a vibrant sense of aliveness, and peace prevailed.

We stopped at Maa Rewa Annashetra for rest. After meditation, we had lunch and rest. Then, we started our journey, and before sunset, we reached Bilgoan. We spent a night staying under a shed in the Monibai Ashramshala campus, a co-education boarding school with around 400 Adivasi (tribal) students. Attendance is compulsory for morning/evening prayer at 6.30 am / 7.00 pm. School timings were from 11.00 am to 5.00 pm, breakfast at 7.30 am, lunch at 10.00 am, and dinner at 6.00 pm. For dinner, we had dal khichari with the children. On request from staff and students, I took a workshop for senior students to prepare them for excellence. The other two parikramawasi continued their journey in the morning - an example of how Narmada Mai helps with resources when required.

Students of the school have been witness to the development of their area during the last few years. Few of them thought that money and worldly wealth were the key factors of life. In contrast, others felt that ethical growth is the key to happiness. Through a story, I conveyed them the importance of vision and moral values.

Parajay was born into a religious, educated, and respectable middle-class family. He was a happy child with a creative brain. He went to Andhra Middle School, around a kilometre from his village. Vijay came from a family of poor farmers. Vijay's father was illiterate and struggled to meet the family's basic needs. Vijay was an undernourished, however intelligent, and fun-loving child. Due to his loving nature and intelligence, villagers loved him and supported his studies. He also went to study at Andhra Middle School. Parajay and Vijay studied in the same class and were toppers in academics and sports. In the sixth class, both got scholarships from the government for higher education in Zila School, Madhubani. Till secondary, both of them fared well in academics. Vijay's friends were devoted to studies, he was highly focused, and his life purpose was to uplift the community. Parajay's friends had an affluent lifestyle and came from mixed backgrounds. Under their influence, Parajay dreamt of becoming a rich man. At undergraduate, Vijay pursued microbiology and got a foreign scholarship to pursue his post-graduation and doctorate in an Ivy League university. Upon completing his studies, he researched and became a known cancer eradication scientist at thirty-five. He has molecules patented in his name. He is happily married with two loving kids, is highly spiritual, spends long hours in spiritual development, and spends most of his spare time in philanthropy work.

Parajay desired to become a rich man in the short term. After secondary education, Parajay entered the real estate business and sold land parcels to doctors, diagnostics centres, and medical shop owners. He earned a fortune, made friends with his clients, and enjoyed evening parties. He got married to a wealthy bride and had two children. Over evening drinks and parties, he became aware of the nexus of rural healthcare operations. He started a healthcare business with the help of a paramedical nurse who acted as a link in the business deals. Financially he did well. Over time he had an extramarital relationship with the nurse. Due to Parajay's drinking behaviour and unethical relationship with the nurse, his wife left him. She took away both the children along with her. Parajay approached his father to sell the land and give him money for his project. Initially, his father was against the proposal and refused to sell his land. However, due to his old age, attachment to his only son, and his wife's insistence, he sold a portion of his property to fund Parajay's project.

Parajay's project started well; however, his focus shifted from the business towards drinking and partying due to his newfound lifestyle. Over a period, he incurred considerable losses in his business and ultimately had to close it. Parajay went into massive debt, and seeing the condition, the nurse also left Parajay and started courting someone else. Due to excessive drinking, Parajay developed severe medical problems in his early forties. Parajay had to sell some of his land to meet his expenses. He started farming on a small plot of the farm. During a hail storm, his field got covered by stones and pebbles. Parajay, seeing stones in his area, went into depression. To meet his expenses, he started working on daily wages. In his spare time, he cleared his field by throwing stones on the road.

One day Krishna, a professional diamond cutter and polisher, was passing through the farm. He recognised that the stones were raw diamonds. So he secretly picked up as much stone he could and, after cutting and polishing them, sold them at a reasonable price to individuals and Mr Diwan, a goldsmith. In turn, the goldsmith presented the polished diamond to the King. On seeing the quality of the diamond, the King acquired Parajay's land after paying him more than market value. Parajay believed King had underpaid and started cursing people who had deceived him and taken raw diamonds away from his fields.

Parajay spent his life pursuing his materialistic dream without understanding the nature of his being (Atma). Though he had plenty in his kitty, he did not come out of his own created miseries and died due to multiple organ failures at the age of forty-five. Many of us are like Parajay. In the darkness of our ignorance, individuals degrade themselves by indulging in sensual pleasure. They only waste precious assets like intelligence, good health, and young age to enjoy trivial pleasures. Only human beings can uplift themselves. Therefore, like Vijay, individuals should use their wisdom and pious actions to enhance spiritual wealth and lasting happiness.

After the workshop at Monibai Ashramshala, I started my journey through the dense forest and steep hills with slippery mud and loose pebbles. One mistake and I could have fallen 500 feet down the mountain. After crossing the ridge to Shelkuvi, Mr Deepak Pawara invited me to his residence. He requested me to have lunch with him, to which I agreed. After lunch, we spent around an hour discussing the importance of parikrama. I left his place around 4.00 pm and reached Dhargoan around 7.00 pm. Dhargoan is a small town having a market, many NGOs, and a farming support centre. I spent the night on the verandah of Shri Somgiri Maharaj, a business owner who had taken diksha (consecration for joining a spiritual cult) to become a Saint around a decade ago. He lives like a Saint. However, he stays at his house and conducts his business as usual. He has built Narmada Mata Temple in front of his house and regularly does puja and aarti. On the top floor of his house, he has an Ashram for parikramawasis. His hospitality was beyond words.

After finishing my morning rituals at Dhargoan, I started my journey around 8.00 am for Khunta Mori. From Dhargoan to Khunta Mori, the road was very steep uphill and strenuous. After lunch and rest at Narmada Sevashram, I reached Mogli around sunset. This stretch has a tar road; many research organisations and NGOs support local farming and skills development. In Mogli, I spent the night with students. At night I had loose motion due to food poisoning. I took medicine in the night and morning. However, my health deteriorated, and the next day I was admitted to Mogli Gramin Hospital with very low blood pressure- 90/60 mm Hg, and uncontrolled loose motion.

With the grace of Narmada Mai, I got admitted to a hospital and became cured. Thanks to the medical facility in the jungle and the dedication of the medical staff, which were commendable. School teachers, doctors, and paramedical staff took good care. I was prescribed oral rehydration salt and injected with saline drip with Metrolonodaz and Meronizadole twice daily for three days. The hospital did not charge me for the treatment and hospitalisation. After regaining my health, I was discharged from the hospital. The nurse attending to me insisted on having lunch since the route forward was tiresome.

After lunch at the hospital, I proceeded to Surgas. Both sides of the road have plenty of bamboo plantations. At Surgas, I had much fun staying with small kids in a school. During dinner, I was surprised to see plenty of kids having represented sports at the national level. Admittedly, the infrastructure for sports could be more robust. Still, their stamina and God-gifted ability have helped these students in athletics and kabaddi.

From Surgas, I came to Vadfali, the border village of Maharashtra and Gujarat. Dr Ratilal was enjoying the afternoon sun rays sitting in his courtyard. We exchanged Narmade Har, and he invited me to his house. He inquired about my experience of parikrama in between patient visits. I enjoyed his hospitality and had excellent fresh snacks (a dish made of flat rice). Dr Ratilal has a long-pending wish to undertake parikrama. However, such a pious journey still needed to be added to his priority list. He excuses himself under the pretext of his busy schedule with patients.

In the afternoon, I left from the Doctor's residence at Vadfali, Maharashtra, crossed the river and entered Gujarat. The road up to Karni was through dense jungles having steep gradients. By early evening I reached Karni. The weather was freezing and windy. On inquiry, I found that five kilometres ahead was Mateshar, and I could cover the distance in an hour. From Karni to Mateshar the climb was extraordinarily steep. With a load of the backpack, it took an extra effort even to put a step forward. Finally, after walking for nearly two hours, I reached the outskirt of the village. I was exhausted, and the intensity of darkness and cold waves increased with the sunset. The village was about two kilometres in length. The Ashram was nearly two kilometres from the village in the forest. With all my efforts, I could not find a place to stay. I was starving and needed food; however, I had to be content with water from a well. Moving forward in the dark through hills, jungle road with loose pebbles and stones, having a steep fall on both sides, with a dim light of a head torch, the sound of winds, probability of animals, and nobody to guide the path became scary. Despite being dead tired, I walked in the darkness for about an hour through the jungle, but no soul was in sight. To my luck, a villager passing by with a block of wood on his head told me that the Ashram was behind two hills.

After dragging myself for some time, I saw the light from a distance, which gave me hope. I shouted Narmade Har, and someone from the other end responded and directed me the way. My torch battery had almost got discharged, nothing was visible, and through sheer instinct, I walked for one and half hours to cross a hill to reach the Ashram around 9.00 pm. In the dense jungle of Shoolpaneshwar (Shoolpani ki Jahri), Sri Nityanand Ashram, Mathasar is thirty feet by thirty feet room made out of wood pillars and thatched by dry leaves. During winters, they burn logs of wood day and night to keep the place warm. With warm water, I freshened myself and sat down near the fire. Since the Ashram is in a jungle, parikramawasis avoid staying there at night. Cooking of food takes place when someone visits for the night. Swami Ji made dinner for both of us, and we had dinner around 10.30 pm. After dinner, to keep ourselves warm, we sat near the fire for some time and then slept. Water for the Ashram comes from the village. We used it very sparingly. Since it was extremely cold and windy, I got up at 7.30 am and finished my morning rituals.

The night struggle was with blessings and awakening. At the crack of dawn, the entire area looked gorgeous. The morning golden rays over green trees, different species of leaves and colours of flowers, and overlapping hills were an art of Divinity. I started feeling the Divine through her magnificent creations. I became sensitive to the blessing of Mai for giving the extraordinary gift of making my travel through Shoolpani ki Jhari (jungle). Newfound wisdom came from trees, flowers, birds, animals and people. Mai has been rewarding me with special talents to fulfil my Divine purpose of existence. I started seeing the rationale of every step during the parikrama. It became a training ground to sharpen my saintly being.

A few parikramawasis and a Saint came to the Ashram in the afternoon. During the discussion about duality in the world, the Saint said existence is complete in itself. Times and situations commit an individual to right or wrong behaviour. From the lens of worldly knowledge, the display of cigarettes in the hands of health enthusiasts shows apparent inconsistency. People expect that health-conscious people will refrain from health-impaired behaviour such as smoking. A stable link between the spiritual attitude and behavioural aspect of sadachar (proper conduct) is necessary for spirituality. Due to the notorious intentional-behavioural gap, people lose faith in the person and the subject.

I asked the Saint what is sadachar. He explained

that social, climate, infrastructure, topography, and behaviour are impactful situational factors that hinder or facilitate individuals' spiritual path. Right action based on fundamentals carried out by generations of awakening through consciousness is known as aachar (right action). Action implemented in the spirit of selflessness to enhance spirituality by respected scholars is sadachar. By practising sadachar, the mind becomes stable. Ego, jealousy, hypocrisy, pride, greed, temptation, lust, and anger get dissolved. After that, mental and neural readiness through moral acts exerts a powerful influence upon individuals' responses to their inner selves rather than objects and outside situations. Such individuals remain grounded in spiritual thoughts, positive evaluations, feelings, and expressions of intentions and observe spiritual actions. He gave examples of Saints who lost spiritual growth due to their known or unknown intention-behaviour gap.

Directives to act or refrain from the action are relevant to an individual searching for appropriate means to gain some desirable object or avoid an undesirable one. A Saint who has attained Brahma Jnana has no unfulfilled personal wants or desires. Having shed self-centred wants, they rejoice only in themselves and are satisfied and content in the self alone. There is nothing to do, nor are they affected by any action. Thus the enlightened Saint stands outside the scrutiny of injunctions. Gajanan Maharaja, Saint from Maharashtra, is regarded as an incarnation of Dattatreya and Lord Ganesh. He expounded on the details of three paths - karma, bhakti, and yoga to attain self-realisation and declared that he follows yoga. He preached yoga but smoked ganja in his long chillum. Today, his Ashram in Shegoan does much work in human development in the areas and attracts thousands of followers every Thursday.

After the lively and awakening session, we had lunch. After that, we started our journey. After a steep climb of seven kilometres through the dense jungle and steep hilly patches, we reached Junwani. The Saint and other parikramawasis stayed back, and I proceeded. The motorable road from Junwani to the main entrance of Shoolpaneshwar Wildlife Sanctuary and a few kilometres to Gora Colony passes through hills and dense forests. The Statue of Unity and its site elevations were visible on the way. The statue seemed to be nearby. On inquiry, I found that the statue was ten kilometres away on the other (Northern) bank of the Narmada. By 5.00 pm, I went to have a darshan of the newly constructed Shoolpaneshwar (He who holds a trident) Mahadev Temple, dedicated to Lord Shiva. The ancient Shoolpaneshwar Mahadev Temple was near Mokhdi village, now submerged in Narmada. Lord Shiva struck his Trishul, and Kashiraj Chitrasen did tapasya at the ancient Temple. As per mythological stories, Lord himself had crafted the Shiva Linga of the old Temple.

I did puja at Shoolpaneshwar Mahadev Temple and then enjoyed the view of Sardar Sarovar Dam and the Statue of Unity. Then, after walking one and a half kilometres, I reached Gora Colony, a large settlement built for the dam project employees, and spent a night at Hari Dham Ashram and Sanskrit School and College. In the evening, students performed aarti and bhajan.

The journey through Shoolpaneshwar (Shoolpani ki Jhari) was a blessing, teaching essential life lessons in an engaging, educating, enduring, and experiential way. Walking alone in the forest boosted my confidence, burned my fear of the unknown to ashes, and enhanced my understanding of the vastness and expanse of nature. With self-discipline, surrender to Narmada Mai, and a focused mind, distraction never came close. I started enjoying the new way of life. Acupressure of the foot while walking on the rough road in cold weather enhanced my strength.

OM Peace, Peace, Peace

Narmade Har.

Virtue

In a small town, a spiritual family with a meagre income lived. Due to famine, nothing grew on the farms. Amarendra, a poor man, took a loan of five hundred rupees on a ten per cent monthly interest from the village landlord. Over three years, the amount increased, and the poor man could not pay it back. The landlord proposed to waive the loan if Amarendra was willing to get his daughter married to him. The poor man's daughter was very clever, smart, and ethical. The father was against the marriage; however, the daughter agreed to marry the landlord if she lost the game. According to the scheme, the landlord had to place a white and a black pebble in the bag. The daughter had to pick a stone from the bag. If she picked a white pebble, the farmer would be free of the loan, and the daughter would be free. If she picked the black stone, the farmer would be free of the loan; however, she would have to marry the landlord.

The daughter was vigilant and noticed that the landlord picked up and placed two black stones in the bag. Then, he asked the daughter of Amarendra to pick up one pebble. She picked up one pebble and dropped it. She apologised to the landlord for dropping the pebble and told him to look into the bag for the one left in the bag. The landlord knew the gravel in the bag was black and did not want to get exposed. Therefore, he waived off her father's loan without any conditions attached. In life, if you are careful, observant, and act smart, you can quickly get rid of the deceiver.

From Gora Colony, I started for Rampara along the bank of Narmada Mai. After taking prasad in Yogananda Ashram, I visited Dashavatar Ranchhodrai Mandir (dedicated to Lord Krishna), constructed in 1923. The priest told me that people recovered the idol from underneath the ground. It beautifully depicts all ten incarnations of Lord Vishnu. In Rampara, Narmada Mai flows in the Northern direction. Narmada Mai flows from South to North between the confluences of the Maine and Keedimankordi rivers. While walking, I saw two crocodiles on the bank of Narmada Mai and plenty of birds flying, catching fish. After walking five kilometres, I had darshan and rested there for a night in Shree Swami Ramanand Sant Ashram. The Ashram has two complexes opposite each other. The Mandir complex has Ram Mandir and Shiva Mandir, a dining hall, and rooms for Sanyasis (Saints) and parikramawasis. Across the road is Bhakt Niwas, to accommodate many devotees from all over the world.

In the Ashram, Shiva Temple has Paras Linga made of mercury, gold, platinum, and other precious material as per guidelines of Trambak established by Lord Vishwakarma. In the evening, there was an elaborate puja and aarti. Devotees assembled in the hall and enjoyed the evening bhajan and aarti. After the aarti, I joined the long queue to have a darshan of Swami Abhiram Das Tyagi. His presence was blissful as if Divinity was flowing out of him. After darshan, I sat in the Mandir and continued meditating for an hour. Then, I went to have Prasad (dinner) in the large dining hall that could accommodate three hundred people. In the morning after aarti, all the devotees had balbhog (breakfast). The discipline and cleanliness of the place were worth noticing. The entire complex was vibrant with peace and calmness.

After walking for two kilometres on the tar road, I took the route along the bank of Narmada Mai. I walked through a marshy, rocky belt followed by farms of a banana plantation. The sight of plenty of birds of different species in swampy land along Narmada Mai made the walk memorable. In Kumbheshwar, after the darshan of Laxmi Ji, I had lunch at Narmada Sewa Ashram. Individuals taking a bath in Kumbheshwar, and after that, in Nashik, Kumbh is blessed twice. After relaxing for some time, I started for Rudh Gaon. Two kilometres from the village was Jalaram Ashram on the banks of the Narmada and Karnjaya River Sangam. Karnjaya is the karma bhumi (place of penance) of Parashurama, Ram, and Ravana. As per mythology, Karja (loans) gets relinquished for people who bathe at the Sangam. By the time I reached the Ashram, the dinner was over. After performing my evening rituals, I went to sleep.

The next day was Narmada Jayanti, the fifth day of the month of Magha (Hindu calendar). Devotees decorated the Narmada Wharf with numerous saffron flags and flowers. People offered sari, bangles, sindoor (vermilion), haldi (turmeric), kumkum (powder used for religious markings) and bhog (food offered to the Gods) to Mai. Kanya (female child) believed to be a daughter of Narmada Mai were invited for Kanya Bhojan (food for small girl child), worshipped, treated to a feast, and offered dakshina. The Ashram organised the function, and many devotees attended it joyfully and with vigour. We went on a procession to bathe in the Sangam in the evening. Hundreds of aarti dia (mud lamps lit with ghee) were floated in the Narmada water as it represents human life.

The next morning, along with four parikramawasis, I crossed the river Karnjaya and reached Sukhdev. Sukhdev is the tapobhumi of Sage Sukhdev and Markande Muni. An impressive four hundred fifty years old Ranshor Temple having a black stone idol is a pointer of the past glory. Then, through pagdandi and inside the banana plantation, we came to Koteshwar Mahadev Ashram, Yoori. After darshan, meditation, lunch and rest, we proceeded to Sita Ram Ashram, Asha, for a night halt. At Gow Ghat, we had the darshan of Gupt Godavari and Deveshwar Mahadev. After that, through a village road and banana plantation, we came to an ancient, vast, and blissful Temple of Mani Nageshwar. In the past, snakes with Mani (gem) had worshipped Lord Shiva in this place to please him. Walking through the field of a banana plantation for a long distance was an exciting experience.

At Mani Nageshwar, a young, calm, and composed Sanyasi doing parikrama was meditating on the veranda overlooking Narmada Mai. I did dandavat pranam (paid obeisance) to the Sanyasi in the evening. He instructed me to sit next to him. After the initial dialogue, I asked him, "How can we remain blissful." He said by surrendering to the Divine and undertaking constant meditation; you will acquire the ability to be within yourself and enjoy blissful living. After the sermon, we both went for the evening aarti, dinner, and meditation. The next morning after taking a bath, we sat for Rudra Puja.

New roads and new parikrama routes were under construction. From Mani Nageshwar, we passed through

Krishna Puri, Rund Gaon, Bhalod, and Prakava to reach Awadhi. At Awadhi, parikramawasis got an invitation to have lunch prasad at a house warming party. After the food and dakshina ceremony of parikramawasis, other guests started having their food. From Awadhi, we came to Jagdish Madhi, a spiritual Temple complex on the bank of Narmada River. In Madhi, the recitation of Ramayana and Ram Dhun has happened 24*7*365 days since last twenty-five years. Due to the mixing of backwater from the sea, Narmada water at Madhi was salty. I could not sleep on the Ashram's verandah due to cold weather and mosquito bites. The next day happened to be Ekadashi. At Jagdish Madhi, Saints and Bhakts were observing fast.

A Saint, parikramawasi, from Kashi, also stayed for the night in Jagdish Madhi. In the morning, I asked him about the importance of Ekadashi. He narrated the sermon of Suta Goswami to the Sages at Nimisharanya to illustrate the benefits of observing Ekadashi's vow. King Rukmangada, the ruler of the world, stayed in Vidisha with his beautiful wife and unmarried son, Dharmangada. He and his family were devotees of Lord Vishnu. They used to chant Lord Vishnu's holy names and observe Ekadashi Vrata (fasting). He also ensured that citizens in his kingdom, from over eight and less than sixty-five years, chanted Lord Vishnu's holy names and observed Ekadashi. People following Ekadashi went to the abode of Lord Vishnu after death. Hell and heaven became practically empty. Yamaraja (Chitragupta), the son of the Sun God, was left with hardly any work. Narada Muni asked Yamaraja why the hell was almost empty. He answered that citizen on earth strictly observe Ekadashi; therefore, everyone attains the Lord's abode after death. Paths leading to my kingdom are vacant since sinful acts of individuals get erased with great endeavour by observing Ekadashi Vrata, and this is the greatness of the Ekadashi Vrata (fast).

Narada Muni and Chitragupta went to Lord Brahma. They told him that due to the fear of King Rukmangada, people on earth only chant Lord Vishnu's holy names and observe Ekadashi Vrata. They do not follow any other religious act. Due to the observance of Ekadashi Vrata, people who have sinned still attain the supreme abode of Lord Vishnu. Therefore, hell was almost empty, and Yamaraja and his assistants had hardly any work.

To help Yamaraja, Lord Brahma created from his mind a gorgeous young woman Mohini. She could agitate thought, arouse lust, cause madness and destroy holy vows. Lord instructed Mohini to approach the King and entice him. After a few years, when the King desires sexual pleasure, tell him not to follow Ekadashi Vrata and forbid citizen of his kingdom to do so, as the observance of a fasting was detrimental to their sensual pleasure. The King may not comply with your wish to abandon the fast on Ekadashi. Then ask the King to cut off his son's head and place it upon your lap. By luring the King and forcing him to quit Ekadashi Vrata, people on the earth will give up fasting on Ekadashi, and hell again will become populated. Following the instruction of Lord Brahma, Mohini descended at Mount Mandara and started singing bhajans near the Shiva Temple.

King Rukmangada was growing old, and as per the custom, he asked his son Dharmangada to accept responsibility for the kingdom and relieve him for the enhancement of his spiritual path. Dharmangada also ensured that everyone worshipped Lord Vishnu and fasted on Ekadashi. After passing the kingdom to his son, to enhance his spiritual quest, King Rukmangada left for Mount Mandara. He saw Mohini, an astonishingly beautiful young lady worshipping the Shiva Linga. After spending a few days in Mandara, the King approached Mohini and proposed to her for marriage. Mohini told the King she was ready to marry him if he promised to fulfil all her wishes without hesitation. The King and Mohini got married with the condition attached.

Rukmangada and Mohini came to the city of Vidisha, where Dharmangada greeted them with respect, accompanied them to the palace, and cared for them with utmost love, compassion, and dedication. Although excessively captivated by Mohini, the King did not give up Ekadashi Vrata. Every two weeks, he would forgo sexual pleasures for three days on Dashami (the tenth day of the lunar cycle). In the ninth year, King Rukmangada shared with Mohini his desire to observe fast in Kartik (Hindu Month) and not indulge in sexual pleasure. Mohini forbade him to keep his vows during the month of Kartik. She reminded him of the promise made to her before marriage.

On the other hand, the King was firm in continuing Ekadashi Vrata and abstaining from sex during Kartik since it is the destroyer of all sins. Since the King did not fulfil her wishes, Mohini got angry and left the palace. Dharmangada was returning to the palace after touring the earth. On the way, he saw Mohini crying and walking away angrily. He asked Mohini the cause of her anger, and she replied that his father was a liar.

Dharmangada assured Mohini that his father was known for his truthfulness. He persuaded her to return to the palace, and Mohini obliged. Dharmangada, with folded hands, asked his father to give Mohini whatever she desired. King Rukmangada narrated to his son the desire of Mohini. Further, he said even if he has to be born as a germ, he will observe Vrata on Ekadashi. After hearing this, Dharmangada called for his mother, Sandhyavali, to mediate and resolve the issue. Sandhyavali requested Mohini to give up her inappropriate demand as the King would not eat cooked food on Ekadashi. Mohini told Sandhyavali that if the King did not wish to dine on Ekadashi, he should give her the head of his son Dharmangada.

On hearing this, Sandhyavali momentarily shivered. On regaining her strength, she said the scriptures clearly state that fasting on Ekadashi should not be abandoned, even at the cost of his wealth, wife, friends, guru, or tapasya.

She was ready to give the head of her son for Mohini's satisfaction. Dharmangada and Sandhyavali persuaded the King not to transgress his vow of truthfulness as they shall certainly attain the favour of Lord Vishnu. Dharmangada took out his sword and placed it before the King, saying, "Cut my head at once and thus keep your promise. Even after the destruction of this body, I will attain another one in due course". The moment the King picked up the sword to kill his son, the earth began to shiver, and the oceans swelled. Hundreds of meteors fell from the sky as raging winds blew, and Lord Vishnu stopped him by catching hold of his arm. Being touched by the Lord's hand, King Rukmangada was immediately free from sinful reactions. Lord Vishnu took all three of them to his eternal abode.

After completing tapasya for twelve years, King Rukmangada's priest, Brahmin Vasu, heard about what had happened. He got furious with Mohini for forcing the King to eat during Ekadashi. He said that this woman was not worthy of living on the earth. He took water in his hand, violently threw it on Mohini, and immediately her body turned to ashes. After death, Mohini was not allowed to enter heaven. Due to the curse of the Brahmin, anyone who touched her got burnt to ashes; therefore, she was tortured even in hell.

King Rukmangada, his wife, and his son had ascended to Vaikunta Loka (Lord Vishnu's celestial abode). After that, fasting on Ekadashi was not observed throughout the world. After death, people went to hell, and Yamaraja got his job back and was thus pleased. Mohini approached Brahma and told her she had nowhere to rest in the three worlds.

Lord Brahma and the other demigods approached Vasu, priest of King Rukmangada. Vasu paid due respects on seeing Lord Brahma and asked them to be seated. The Lord narrated the entire story and requested Vasu to be compassionate with Mohini. Vasu gave up his anger and told Lord Brahma that Mohini was unfit to live with others due to her sinful contamination. Therefore, let her live in a deserted place. At Lord Brahma's request, the Brahmin consented to restore Mohini's body. The Brahmin sprinkled water from his water pot onto Mohini's ashes, and immediately, she acquired a physical form. Mohini bowed down to her father and the Brahmin Vasu. Mohini requested the Lord to grant her the power to observe Ekadashi. Mohini started fasting on Ekadashi and got salvation.

After the sermon, we went for Ekadashi bhog (food offered to God). After the bhog, we visited Guman Dev, an ancient pilgrimage (tapobhumi) Temple complex dedicated to Ram Bhakt Hanuman. The Temple has a large swayambhu (self-created) idol of Lord Hanuman. The complex was huge and well-maintained. On Hanuman Jayanti, during the sacred month of Shravan (Hindu Calander), numerous bhakts come to take darshan at Guman Dev and a big mela is organised. There was a long queue for the darshan at the Temple, and I had to wait for one hour. After the darshan, we proceeded to Ankleshwar and spent a night in Ram Kund, a vast Temple complex on the outskirts of Ankleshwar.

From Ankleshwar, I went to Bulbula Kund, Rishi Kashyap's Tapobhumi. In Bulbula Kund (pond), as you shout Narmade Har, the water rises in a fountain formation and recedes. After lunch and some rest, we came to Rudra Kund, Sajod, and had the darshan of Siddrarashwar Tirtha and Khapar Mata. Rudra Kund (pond) had big tortoises of different species. People feed puffed rice to tortoises and enjoy seeing them. From Rudra Kund, we started our journey for Suraj Kund. On the way, a bhakt offered tea/snacks and requested me to spend the night at their place. Since Suraj Kund was around two kilometres only, and being a tirtha, I decided to spend a night there. At around 7.30 pm, I reached Surya Kund, Hanset. The market was closed, and I had to sleep without proper dinner. After taking a bath the next morning, I had the darshan of Hansheswar- Tileshwar - Ratneshwar Mahadev and then proceeded to Bimleshwar.

From Guman Dev to Bimleshwar, the tar road was in excellent condition. Many oil rigs of ONGC are visible in the area. In Bimleshwar, I had the darshan of Narmada Mandir and five Swayambhu (self-created) Shiva Lingas. I got myself registered to cross the sea the next morning. Only three Parikramawasi had arrived, and there was a doubt regarding the next day's trip. Ferry service was available only if fifty yatris (people on pilgrimage) gets registered. By 8.00 pm, one hundred twenty people during parikrama in buses arrived. I went to the registration counter in the morning. Officials verified my parikrama credential and aadhaar card. I paid one hundred rupees as ferry charges to cross the confluence (sangam) where Narmada Mai merges in Rewa Sagar (Gulf of Khambhat / Arabian Sea) and sails further to Mithitalia. Being Purnima, I fasted and did dhyana (meditation), whereas other parikramawasis went for bhandara (feast). After feast parikramawasis got dakshina by the devotees travelling in a bus and private vehicles. We left Bimleshwar around noon and walked two kilometres by road to reach the shore.

We had to walk another five hundred metres through slippery and muddy water to catch the ferry at the shore. We waited for the boat for about an hour. Three ships left Bimleshwar for Mithitalia around 2.15 pm. Many parikramawasis travelling by bus from Pune were sitting around me in the boat. After the initial introduction, the experience of doing parikrama on foot and the journey through Shoolpani ki Jhari was the subject of discussion. They gave me dry fruits to eat since I was fasting. Luckily the sea was calm, and we enjoyed the journey. We performed the required Rewa Sagar and Narmada Mai rituals at the Sangam. I offered payer, narial (coconut), supari (beatle), janua (sacred thread) to the sea and chunri (red decorated cloth), sindoor (vermilion), bangles, and rice to Narmada Mai. We had a group photo on debarking at Mithitalia around 5.15 pm; a few stayed back, and others left for Baruch.

The Law of nature taught me that people would get attracted and leave you at an appropriate time. With dignity, welcome them and gracefully allow them to depart. At times, I could not stick to the plan and had to wait for the appropriate time to move forward. Initially, I got irritated, but parikrama taught me that an obstacle or injury is either a safety check or a capability test for moving forward. Steep terrain, uneven roads, and walking through the jungle taught me many life lessons. I learned to walk my life path with appropriate restraints, self-discipline, and mantra chanting, keeping the mind focused on the "now". I felt energetic by observing bhakti and controlling vairagya and negative thoughts. I got absorbed in my purpose and immersed in ethical actions without being distracted by unrelated, trivial, and peripheral issues. In such a state of bliss, a sense of space and time slowed down. I moved forward with grace and dignity, without ego, head held high and feet on the ground.

OM Peace, Peace, Peace

Narmade Har.

Grace

For an individual, it is best to do something good immediately and avoid unethical work and behaviour having adverse consequences. A boat ferrying a wealthy trader in the river Ganga got stuck in a whirlpool and started sinking. The trader started shouting for his life. He told the boatmen to save him, and he would give him half of his property in return. The boatman put all his skills and could sail through the spiral. As the boat moved to calm water, the trader thought it foolish to part with half his property. The boatman has just done his duty; otherwise, he would have sinned by not performing his task. The boatman smilingly rowed the boat to the shore. On reaching the coast, the trader gave him ten rupees for snacks. The smiling boatman said God takes care of me. It was my duty to ferry you safely, and I have done the same. Thank you.

On reaching Mithitalia, I bathed in the sea and the well water at Krishnanand Ashram. Industrial units of Dahej surround the Ashram. After the bath, I had a darshan of Limbeshwar Mahadev. Later in the evening, all parikramawasis performed puja and aarti. The area is widespread; however, the facilities and upkeep needed attention. Unfortunately, the caretaker was least interested in maintaining the site. Plenty of mosquitoes and insects were in the rooms, and we could not sleep. I with another parikramawasi started our journey the next morning after doing aarti and puja. On the way to Abhata, we ate sattu (a dry powder mixture of ground pulses and cereals) and drank milk in Krishnamurti Ashram. In the afternoon, we rested in Somnath Mahadev Mandir, Suwa Gaon. By evening we reached Kacerole and spent the night at Narmada Mandir, situated within the township.

On the way to Bharuch, a milkman bhakt, sitting by the road, stopped us and offered matha (buttermilk). He told his wife to prepare fresh parathas and vegetables for us. His son had a mental disorder and slept all day. By evening we reached Shankaracharya Math, Bharuch. In the Ashram, we stayed overnight under a tin shed. My wife came from Mumbai to hand over a few articles. The next morning the Saint in the Ashram prepared delicious food. After offering it to the Lord, he served lunch to all parikramawasis. My wife left Baruch around 11.00 am. After some rest, we went for darshan at Ram Mandir and Gayatri Mandir. We proceeded to Neelkanth Mahadev Mandir, Jhareswar, spread across many acres. Passengers doing parikrama on buses arrived at the complex to spend a night, performed aarti and sang bhajans in groups. The Temple trust served dinner to parikramawasis, who came on foot.

Next morning after puja and aarti, we proceeded to Shukla Tirtha. En route at Karod, we had the darshan of Koteshwar Mahadev. Shukla Tirtha is an ancient spiritual village with numerous old temples. Mahadev Mandir (mentioned in Narmada Puran), Ram Mandir, Hunkarnath (Vishnu) Mandir, Mangaleshwar Mandir, and Dutta Mandir are a few important temples we visited. We received an invitation to have lunch at a marriage ceremony. After lunch, we went to the bridegroom's house, blessed him, and proceeded to Dharmasheela. We spent the night at Sai Dham Ashram, between the main road and Narmada Canal.

In the evening satsang, the discussion revolved around the Divines' golden gifts - samay (time), socha (good thoughts), vivek (discretion), and satsang (spiritual discourse). Mind, intellect, memory and ego define our behaviour. Parikrama unites individuals with nature and the Divine. It inculcates internal changes to know the Self, erases negativity, enhances correctness and tears down the ego. It is possible only when you have bhava (devotion), bhajans (songs in praise of God), bhavana (feeling of joy), and union with Bhagwan (God).

The next day we planned to stay at Ojha, where Kunti and her sons had done tapasya. During Mahabharata, Ojha was named Chota (small) Ayodhya. At Ojha, people can find idols of God and Goddesses in Narmada Mai. Every twelve years, pilgrims gather in massive numbers in this place. At Ojha, we stayed on the first floor of Puneet Ashram. The complex is on the bank of Narmada. It has temples of Lord Shiva (eleven in number), Hanuman, Narmada, and Ganesh. The Ashram was re-established by Puneet Maharaja, who did tapasya under the banyan tree, which stands tall on the front lawn of the complex. From the complex terrace, the Moon's reflection in the Narmada was a delight and worth seeing.

In the evening discourse, a Saint vividly described Lord Shiva. Lord Shiva appears as an ascetic clad in a loincloth or tiger skin. He is the Adi Guru, having all the powers acquired by meditation, penance, and a life of austerity. The Lord is the destroyer of impurities, illusion, and imperfection. He is the demolisher of ego, moha (attachment), kama (lust), and krodha (anger). The Lord spreads love and liberates his pure-hearted disciples from the cycle of birth and death. To save the good from evil, he consumed the halahal (a deadly poison), which emerged during the churning of the ocean by Gods and demons.

Lord Shiva is the source of many spiritual and material sciences and arts, like yoga, meditation, medicine, science, dance, etc. The entire universe manifests itself in His meditating consciousness.

1. His third eye represents Divine omniscience, wisdom, and insight
2. A crescent moon on top of His hair represents the cyclical nature of time
3. Three horizontal lines of vibuthi (white ash) on His forehead represent an all-pervading nature
4. Agni represents the fire of destruction
5. The Celestial River Ganga flowing from His matted locks represents sanctity and purity, strength and prosperity, essential instruments of ritual purification
6. The Cobra snake around His neck shows him as a power of destruction and creation
7. The axe represents His militancy nature
8. Damru (hand drum) represents the cosmic sound
9. OM is the primordial sound
10. Antelope as animal usefulness
11. Body smeared with ashes sitting in yogic posture with a Trishul /trident represents supreme knowledge, karma, devotion, creation, preservation, and destruction

12. Shiva Lingam represents the seed of the universe and a protective power at the origin of all beings

13. Yoni, the round base of Shiva Lingam, represents Shakti or female power. It symbolises the interaction between male and female power to balance the reconciling force of the universe

14. Ardhanareshwar - half of Lord Shiva's and half of Goddess Parvati's body symbolises equality and synthesis between masculine and feminine energies as the root of all creation.

Along the Narmada Bank and in many parts of the country, there are innumerable pilgrimages and temples of Lord Shiva and his wife, Uma, also known as Parvati. On Saint's advice, I meditated on Lord Shiva in the Temple complex and felt blessed, fresh, and energetic. Calmness prevailed, and many negative memories got erased.

From Ojha, we came to Nareshwar, tapobhumi (place of tapasya) of Saint Shree Rang Avadhuta. Saint Shree Rang Avadhuta Temple complex on the bank of Narmada has a serene and beautiful ambience. It has the Mandir of the Saint Shree Rang Avadhuta, a museum preserving the Saint's belongings, a book store selling all the publications of the Saint, and a guest house. It is maintained very nicely in its original form. In the complex, all the devotees had prasad. After darshan, we proceeded to Sankat Mochan Tapowan Dham, Kahona, and Siddhi Yog Ashram, Daroli. We walked along the bank of Narmada Mai from Dorali to Marhi. Many temples are under construction along the route.

The area around Ojha is very fertile. The plantation of flowers (roses), bananas, sesame oil, cotton, chilli, dal, and vegetables was visible. Villagers have plenty of cows, buffaloes, and goats. They feed them with green grass, cabbage, and other green plants. Due to less water flow from the dam, Narmada Mai flows like a canal. Through cross-country farm and village roads, we reached Malsar, a renowned spiritual place in Gujarat with temples of Mangalnath Mahadev (Angareshwar), Audika Mata, and Panch Mukhi Hanuman. Aurangzeb wanted to destroy Mangalnath Mahadev Temple when fire from the sky wrecked the army. Therefore, it is known as Angareshwar Mahadev. Sinner Town is an old spiritual centre. From Malsar, we went to Sinner and felt blessed after the darshan of the eighth Shiva Mandir and a Ganesh Mandir.

From Sinner along the Narmada River, we walked through the thorny bushes and pagdandi to Annusuia Mata. Annusuia is on the bank of Aarandi and Narmada Sangam. Aarandi River had dried. The saying goes that the mud of the Sangam cures all skin ailments. I also applied the soil on my right foot, having skin irritation, which also worked for me. This place is tapobhumi of Annusuia Mata. She was very pious and always practised austerity and devotion. She was the wife of Maharishi (supreme Sage) Atri and mother of Lord Dattatreya (an incarnation of Vishnu), Sage Durvasa (an incarnation of Shiva), and Chandratri (an incarnation of Brahma). In Annusuia, we stayed in a shed lacking electricity and basic amenities. I was hungry, all the stalls were closed, and no food was available. Around 10.00 pm, a parikramawasi woke me up and asked me to share food since villagers had prepared extra food for him. I readily agreed. It rained the whole night, and mosquitoes had free time. The next morning, I had a darshan of Lord Dutta, Annusuia Mata, and Gupt Ganga. After finishing our morning rituals at sunrise, we proceeded to Badrika

Ashram, tapobhumi of Swami Girishanand. After the darshan of Badrinarayan and Kedarnath Mahadev, we walked along Narmada Bank to Chandood. This place has ancient Shejesh Shahi Narayana (magnificently carved idol of Lord Vishnu in a sleeping pose and Goddess Lakshmi standing at his feet), Kedarnath Mahadev, Anandmata and Dutta Mandir.

After darshan and puja at Badrika Ashram, we walked along the Narmada bank to Dakshin Prayag Triveni Sangam (confluence of three rivers Narmada, Orsang, and Gupt Saraswati), Karnali. On the way, I tripped over a stone, had a fall and sprained my left knee. Fellow parikramawasi helped me and gave me water. I was unable to stand up. I applied the oil given by Tel Wala Baba and slowly, crossing the Orsang River, walked to Karnali. Karnali is a city of temples with six ghats – the famous being Malhar Rao Ghat. On Purnima, thousands of devotees come to the ghats for a holy dip. Bhakts perform sraddha (rituals after death) and different religious functions. After bathing in Sangam, we came to Kuber Bhandari – Kubershwar Mandir. Lord Kuber had built this Temple. At Karnali, taking a bath in Sangam and having darshan and prasad (food offered to the Lord of the Temple) is auspicious. Every day hundreds of devotees have their food in the Kuber Bhandari Temple free of cost. I was fortunate to have darshan at Mahadev Mandir, Kali Mandir, and Shakti Peeth.

We slept on the veranda of Kubeshwar Mahadev Temple (known as Kuber Bhandari). The night was cold and windy, and the terrace was open from three sides. Early morning, after bathing at the Prayag Triveni Sangam, we had darshan of several mandirs at Karnali. As I could barely walk, I took medicine and rested for two days on

Doctor's advice at Shree Yantra Shakti Peeth, Karnali. Other parikramawasis left for Tilakwada.

After taking two days' rest at Karnali, I came to Moriya. After meditation, lunch, and rest at Hanuman Mandir, I visited Tilakwada (a tehsil town in Narmada District). I went to the Government Hospital for an examination. The Doctor gave me medicines for three days and called me for further investigation the next day. I spent the night at Vasudev Saraswati Kutir. On my way to the hospital the following morning, I had the darshan of Mani Nageshwar, Kapileshwar, and Kameshwar Mahadev. After the darshan, I visited the hospital for a medical examination. They took samples of blood and urine. All the reports of blood tests were in the normal range. The Doctor was astonished to see healthy metrics; however, he gave me medicines free of cost for thirty days as a precautionary measure.

From Tilakwada, I came to Gurudaspur. Construction of the dam across the Narmada River was in full swing, so the area was polluted and needed to be more organised. From Gurudaspur, I had an excellent view of the Statue of Unity. I spent a night in room K6, Dutta Mandir Guest House. Dutta Mandir is a massive complex with different types of accommodations and dining spaces. I had the darshan of Koteshwar, Naradeshwar, Dutta Mandir, and Samadhi of Swami Vasudev Saraswati, who is considered an incarnation of Lord Dutta.

Swami Vasudev Saraswati left his body in 1914 AD on the bank of Narmada Mai in Gurudaspur. He followed Dutta Sampradaya and authored nineteen holy books on spirituality. In the evening, we went to the main dining hall for dinner, which can accommodate approximately five hundred persons at a time. After dinner, we started discussing the essence of Swami Vasudev Saraswati's teaching.

The primary objective of human life is to obtain moksha (liberation from cycles of birth and death). To purify the mind, an individual needs to be ethical while pursuing any means of livelihood. People need to be aware of their spiritual obligations, varna (level of spiritual growth), and the stage of life. Commitment to spiritual development is a must. A purified mind helps in upasana (progress towards their higher Self) and brings peace and calmness. A peaceful mind has the potential to become aware of the real Self, the sole means of liberation. Temptation of mind is the creation of Maya. The steadiness of the mind comes from shravana (studying /listening to discourses of realised Saints), the study of Vedanta (conclusion of Vedas), bhajans (devotional songs), manana (contemplation), and nididhyasana (meditation). A pure, wholesome, moderate diet helps cultivate a sattvic (serene, harmonious, balanced) nature. A steady mind leads to faith and observance of spiritual conduct.

Snaan (bath), sandhya (prayer) and Dev Puja (worship of Gods) add flavours to an individual's spiritual being. Every human should practice the five significant yajnas (that which purifies, heals and relaxes our life, mind, and actions) - devotion, sacrifice, offering, restraint, and kirtan (narrating /reciting spiritual scriptures) to help unite, have a sense of connection and unity with the Divine. Atithti satkar (honour to the guest), soft and kind speech, refraining from harming anyone in any way; service and obedience to parents, spouse, in-laws and other elders help build a sattvic mind. We sang few bhajans and then went to our rooms. The next morning, I went for a bath in Narmada

Mai. Then I went for a darshan and puja to Dutta Mandir, Mahadev Mandir and Mata Ji ki Mandir.

From Gurudaspur, I came to Panch Mukhi Hanuman Mandir, Airia. On the side of the road is the Temple complex. At the Temple, a Swami Ji gives free medicines to devotees. I was tired and slept in the hall for some time. Later in the afternoon, I walked to Choti Ambaji Mandir, Undwan. The decoration of the Mandir was beautiful. Different varieties of sweets and dishes were in preparation for the Shivaratri festival. In the evening, many devotees and Saints sang bhajans in the complex. Late at night, we had a very delicious meal and sweets. The next day was Shivaratri, and I fasted.

Since early morning there was a long queue of devotees offering flower garlands with mango leaves, fruits or sweets, and water on Shiva Linga and Durga Mata. I enquired from a learned Brahmin, who had just finished his darshan and puja, about the significance of these offerings. The Brahmin replied that offering to God brings blessings for lasting happiness, compassion, peace of mind, and a healthy body. In the Gita, Lord Krishna says param (leaves), pushpam (flowers), phalam (fruits), toyam (water), yome bhaktya prayachchhati (offer it with devotion). People offer leaves, flowers, fruits, and water with love and devotion in spiritual practices. I asked him what lesson we should take from Shivaratri. He replied that with all the divinity of Narmada Mai, sand within her remains as sand and does not transform into water. Similarly, individuals with negative memories are jealous, hateful and inert.

An individual has to become useful and accomplishing as a leaf is to the tree and environment. The leaf converts the sunlight into food for the tree. It inhales carbon dioxide, exhales oxygen, releases excess water, and provides food and air to help the plant grow and stay healthy. Similarly, people should convert external energy into positive food for the mind, heart, and body. Be positive despite being surrounded by negativity, and through forgiveness, release excess negative baggage of the past. Flowers feed many species, provide natural medicines, aid in plant reproduction, and add beauty to nature. Individuals should also be useful to others, offer spiritual and ethical living globally, help build a healthy society and spread peace, calmness, and happiness.

Fruit is a healthy diet, reduces the risk of chronic disease and is a source of many nutrients. Similarly, individuals should have healthy mental, emotional, and physical dispositions. It helps to remain calm, composed, and positive; be healthy by moving away from lust, anger, and greed. They provide spiritual nutrients to themselves and their surroundings.

Water is vital for life, as the saying is, "No water, No life." Rivers flow through turbulent waterfalls and huge rocks, yet it finds their way to her destination. It helps the entire basin for drinking, recreation, industry, agriculture, energy production, and spiritual practices. It acts as a centrepiece of the environmental canvas. Water is soft and flexible and can mix and adapt to the properties of others.

Similarly, people should be gentle, patient, humble, flexible, and accommodating to remain happy. They should be persistent in cutting through layers of Maya, devoted enough to merge with the Divine, and generous to let others grow. When people offer themselves to the Divine through devotion as leaves, flowers, fruits, and water, they become softer and more flexible than water.

Every moment is a new moment; experience the newness. It is only possible if you leave the space for newness to enter yourself. Therefore, move ahead with the wish to transform yourself, and the Divine shall bless you with everlasting bliss.

Narmada Mai cares for all her devotees irrespective of class, caste, religion, age or knowledge. People residing and doing Parikrama of the Narmada Mai are always blessed. Do your best and leave the result to Narmada Mai. When time is good, devotees thank her by offering prasad, and in the bad times, they pray to her for blessing and seek forgiveness for their wrong deeds. It is only a matter of time before unpleasant situations turn around for good. During parikrama, miracles happen all the time. At times I enjoyed the best of the hospitality, even at odd hours and in bad weather conditions, and other times had to forego my meals. I felt blessed in the company of Narmada Mai. Generally, devotees offer prasad to Saints. Along Narmada Bank, Saints and bhakts prepare food, serve parikramawasis, and fulfil their necessities.

OM Peace, Peace, Peace

Narmade Har.

Knowledge

A farmer used to sell one kilogram of cow ghee to the local vegetable vendor every month. The vendor weighed the ghee to see if he was getting the right quantity, and to his surprise, he found that it was underweight. He got angry and tried to argue with the farmer for a refund. The farmer refused to pay the money; therefore, the vendor took the matter to the village Panch (jury). The Panch members asked the farmer why he gave the vendor less ghee. The farmer replied, "I am poor and illiterate. I have a scale, but I do not have a proper measure". The Panch asked the farmer to produce the weight he used to weigh ghee. The farmer replied that "Before the vendor started buying ghee from me, I had been purchasing a kilogram of potato from him. When the vendor brings the potato, I put it on the scale and give him the same weight in ghee." If anyone was at fault, it was the vendor. In life, everything that goes out comes back.

After having puja and darshan of Mata Ji, Mahadev, and Vishwanath Baba in Ambaji, I came to Boriyad through a village dirt road. I rested on the veranda of Rajeshri Shop and, after that, proceeded to Bhaka along the State Highway. At Shiva Mandir, Bhaka celebration of Shivaratri, the recitation of bhajans and shlokas and the attire of bhakts presented a festive ambience. Pandits conducted

Rudra Abhishek in the Shiva Mandir, which finished around 9.30 pm. Saint Govardhan Giri Maharaja performed puja throughout the night, and girls/women sang bhajans. All newly married couples dressed in local costumes and ornaments witnessed the ceremony throughout the night. I also had the privilege of doing abhishek at midnight, which is considered auspicious. The next day I got phalhari (auspicious food) for lunch.

I inquired about the significance of observing a fast on Shivaratri from Maharaj Ji. He illustrated the importance of Shivaratri through a mythological story. Out of the illicit relationship of a Brahmin widow with a chandala (wicked individual), a son named Dussah was born. He was a man of unethical character - he used to gamble, drink, commit robbery, and murder. On the day of Shivaratri, he went to a Shiva Temple to commit robbery. He remained awake all night for an appropriate opportunity but could not steal the Temple property. In the crowded Temple, people sang devotional songs and worshipped the Shiva Linga the entire night. He spent his time listening to the Divine stories of Lord Shiva. Since he had listened to stories of Lord Shiva the whole night, in his next birth, he was born into a family of King Chitrangad and was named Vichitraveerya. With his devotion to Lord Shiva, Vichitraveerya ultimately united with Him and manifested as Veerabhadra. Similarly, King Bharat, Mandhata, Dhundhumar, Harishchandra, and many other devotees of Lord Shiva have attained salvation by observing Shivaratri's fast. People who worship Lord Shiva get rid of their sins.

I stayed in Bhakha for four days and enjoyed doing sewa and satsang. We cleaned the entire place and did bhajans and puja as per Vedic practices. I practised meditation in the hall early in the morning and late evening. I also got myself examined by a homoeopathic doctor who gave me medicines and advised rest. Saint Gowardhan Giri Maharaja treated my leg with Akaka patta (leaf of Blue Madar plant). From Bhaka along the state highway, I came to Chaparia (Knawat). I had lunch at Narmada Parikrama Ashram. By the evening, I reached Neelkanteshwar Mahadev Mandir, Kadipani. Kadipani is a beautiful place surrounded by lush green hills. The bauxite factory had been closed, and the town looked abandoned. Swami Ji at the Ashram was very helpful. He prepared excellent cuisine for all the parikramawasis. He had satsang with all of us staying in the Ashram. The next morning after puja and aarti, I had Mahadev Ji's darshan and proceeded to Hafeshwar.

Considering the steep gradients from Kadipani to Hafeshwar, walking with my luggage would be tedious. On the advice of Swami Ji, I left my backpack and went to Hafeshwar (District Chhota Udepur). One has to go through the jungle, having hills with steep climbs and slopes. While travelling to Hafeshwar, people experience breathlessness; hence the place is known as Ha-fesh-war (the Hindi word for panting). Hafeshwar was a scenic place surrounded by Narmada Mai and jungles from three sides. Narmada Mai was full of water, and the Temple's architecture was grandeur.

The original Hafeshwar Mandir got submerged in Sardar Sarovar Dam. The Shiva Linga has a bargad (banyan) tree (grown from the Shiva Linga). The Hanuman idol retrieved from the old Temple is in the new Temple. Idols of Kalhenshwar Mahadev, Sita Ram, Radha Krishna, Durga, and Narmada Mai are new. Markande Rishi, in conversation with Yudhirsthir, narrated the story of Kalhans Rishi, who was doing tapasya of Lord Shankar (Shiva). Indra came to test him. The Rishi told him he wanted the darshan of Lord Shiva. With the blessing of Indra, the Rishi had the darshan of Lord Shiva. The Rishi requested Lord Shiva to reside in this place, hence the Lord is known as Kalhanseshwar Mahadev. After a bath in Narmada Ji and darshan at the Mandir, I had lunch at the Temple guest house. At around 4.00 pm, I started from Hafeshwar and returned for a night stay in Kadipani.

Kadipani is on the border of Gujarat and Madhya Pradesh. Taking pagdandi (road suitable for walking only), I crossed the hills to enter Madhya Pradesh and, through the rough track, walked for around ten kilometres to reach Vakhatgarh. I had fresh tomatoes and papad (papadum) in the village. After walking for another four kilometres, I reached Kali Mandir, Umari. At the Mandir, I meditated, had lunch and rested. The path from Umari to Umarat has multilayer scattered hills, taller ones at the back and smaller hillocks in the front. Occasionally few houses were seen on a hilltop. Villages are a few kilometres apart. The golden shadow of the sunset on hills and small houses had a beautiful panoramic view. In Umarat, I stayed at a farmhouse of a devotee. After taking a bath and performing meditation, puja and aarti, we discussed parikrama, local culture, farming, crops, and education in the valley. At around 9.00 pm, all of us had an excellent dinner.

From Umarat, through broken and rocky roads, along the valley with hills and fertile land on both sides, I came to Gulwat. The land across the route is very fertile and apt for wheat crop. I had balbhog (breakfast) in Temla at Mr Purushottam Rathore's house. After a little rest, I crossed the Hatni River to reach Kawada. After resting under a tree shade in Hanuman Mandir, I had my routine check-up in a mobile clinic in front of the Mandir gate. I had swollen legs and blood pressure. The nurse gave me medicines and vitamin tablets. Medical service was free. I came to the Temple, and as I was ready to proceed further, the priest brought some delicious snacks and sweets, which I enjoyed.

I left Kawada around 3.30 pm, and by 6.20 pm, I reached Dahi. I spent the night on the veranda of the Hanuman Mandir. Dahi is a small town, and on the outskirts is a Hanuman Temple with a large complex and well-maintained garden full of roses and seasonal flowers. In the Temple, Ram Dhun is on 24*7*365 days. I had a darshan of idols of Lord Shiva, Hanuman, Radha Krishna, and Guru Sthan of Kamal Das Ji Maharaj. In the evening, many devotees gathered for aarti. Devotees sang bhajans (spiritual songs), and others followed their tune.

After dinner, at around 9.00 pm, I went to wash my plate and got puzzled to see a young boy engaged in weight lifting in the Temple's backyard. On talking to him, I learned that he came from a very poor background. Mandir management takes care of all his requirements. During the day, he goes to his college and, after that, to private tuition. In the morning and evening, he helps in the kitchen and upkeep of the Mandir. He was passionate about weightlifting. Since he was only free at night, Mahant Ji (Saint of the Mandir) personally trains him according to his suitability. He has won many awards at the state level.

Early morning after aarti and puja, I left for Koteshwar. A bhakt provided lunch en route on his farm, and by 6.00 pm, I reached Kanak Bihari Mandir, Koteshwar. After taking a bath in the Narmada, I performed puja and aarti. The next morning, along the road, I came to Chikaldha, and due to the hot weather, I stopped at a Pathan Shop on the side of the highway. Since the temperature was hot, I decided to sleep on a veranda, having a tin shed next to his shop. Mr Pathan is a Muslim but a devotee of Narmada Mai. He serves all parikramawasis passing through the road.

After resting, through the bank of Narmada Mai, I came to Malwada and had darshan and prasad in Hanuman Mandir. In the late afternoon, I left Malwada and reached Bodhwada. An eleventh-century Lord Shiva Temple known as Devpath Linga Mahadev (described in Narmada Purana) or Deveshwar (described in Shiva Mahapuran) is in the village. God and Goddess started Narmada Parikrama from this holy Temple. Lord Vishwakarma built this Temple, and the Pandavas established the Devpath Lingas. It had twelve Shiva Lingas. Two Lingas are in the Mandir premise, one in the village, and nine got submerged in the Narmada. One Shiva Linga is inside the Mandir built on Shri Yantra and has Rudra Yantra at the top. Raja Bali restored this Temple around 2200 years back. It has thirty six feet high gumbad (top structure on Mandir). I had snan (bath) in the Narmada Mai and retired on the Temple's veranda for the night. The entire night I was alone in the Mandir as villagers left after the evening aarti.

The next morning, I went to the village and had a darshan of Mahadev Ji inside a residential house. After having balbhog (breakfast), I advised Mr Mukesh's son and helped him choose the right career. His elder son was pursuing a Bachelor of Engineering from Indore. The younger one needs to improve his studies but requires help to complete a basic course in automobile mechanics from the nearby Industrial Training Institute.

I walked around nine kilometres to reach Ma Rewa Kutir, Pamela. After darshan, I had ground nuts and jaggery for lunch and rested for two hours. In the afternoon, I walked along the Narmada for around fourteen kilometres to reach Bardha. Up to Perkhad, the area was rocky, and after that, the land was very fertile. In Bardha, I bathed in the Narmada Mai, had darshan and night halt at Mahakaleshwar Mandir. Early morning, I left from Bardha. After crossing the Chiri River, I visited Sukhleswar, a Mahadev Temple on the hilltop in Kothara village. No one was there in the Temple, but the gates were open. Since the outside temperature was around forty degrees centigrade, I spent the afternoon in the Mandir and then started walking.

As I walked, a businessman requested me to spend a night at Vakratunda Ganesh Mandir, Paraga. The Mandir is built next to the road and is known for its spiritual powers. He arranged dinner for me and other parikramawasis from his house. I have been suffering from constipation for the last few days. Due to exertion, my feet got swollen. I had a sound sleep, and early morning, I felt relieved of my constipation and leg pain. What a miracle!

From Ganesh Mandir, another old parikramawasi started walking along with me. By lunchtime, we reached the base of Mandav Hills through the village dirt road. We had lunch and rest at Bal Sarup Hanuman Mandir, located in the jungle next to the road leading to Mandawgarh. After resting for an hour, we proceeded to Mandawgarh (Mandu). Mandawgarh was six kilometres from the base. A connecting cement road with a very steep elevation led up to the top of the plateau.

Mandawgarh, or Mandu, is an ancient city from the 6th century AD, situated at six hundred thirty-three meters (2,079 feet) on the Vindhya Range. To the North of Mandu is the plateau of Malwa. In the South is the valley of the Narmada River. Neelkanth Mahadev Temple on the outskirts of Mandu is dedicated to Lord Shiva and has elegant Mughal designs carved out of large stones. An idol of Neelkanteshwar Mahadev is in the garbha griha (sanctum sanctorum) of the Temple facing the holy pond.

After the darshan of Mahadev, we came to Chaturbhuj Shri Ram Mandir, which is around eleven hundred years old. It is the only Mandir where Ram has four hands. The Lord holds a bow in the upper left hand; in the right hand is an arrow; the hand underneath the bow holds sankha (conch); under the hand is an arrow holding a mala (beads). Near the right side, at Lord Rama's feet, is the idol of Hanuman, and on the other side is Angad. Seven monkeys are sitting at the base. An idol of a monkey named Neel is at Lakshman's feet. Priests had hidden all the idols of the Ram Mandir in a cave when Aurangzeb tried to destroy the Mandir. A Saint from Pune had sapna (dream), and he narrated the same to the Queen of Mandu, who rebuilt the Mandir in 1805 AD. In Mandu, we stayed at Sai Mandir. At night, there was a music and dance performance by the Bhil community on the occasion of Bhaguria, a pre-Holi (colour festival) celebration.

A new Temple is where Markandeya Muni had built Markandeya Mahadev Temple. After the darshan of Mahadev, we proceeded to Rewa Kund through the lush green jungle and the steep climb. The Queen used to come to her palace opposite the kund for the darshan of Narmada Mai, which flows fifteen kilometres away from the kund. Pleased by the Queen, Narmada Mai came near her castle, in the form of a kund and hence it was named Rewa Kund. Dhanod is around three thousand feet below Rewa Kund, and we had to climb down three kilometres, crossing two hills. I had to navigate through an extremely difficult, steep downhill, zigzag, slippery slope with small, loose pebbles and large stones. On the way, I saw a few large lakes in the plain. In one place, my shoes slipped due to wobbly rocks, and I had a fall. Luckily, I was able to catch a bush and got saved. I paid gratitude to Narmada Mai and slowly climbed down.

In the plain we took the road to Bagwania and came to Chitrakoot Akhand Sachidanand Ashram. After lunch, we rested in a shed next to the newly constructed Mandir. In the afternoon, my colleague parikramawasi stayed back, and I proceeded to Dhanod and spent a night at Hanuman Mandir. My shoes had worn out, and I got the same repaired from Sanjay Shoe Hospital. The next morning I walked to Maheswar along the highway. I walked towards the riverfront after having fruits in the shade of the bus stand. On the way, a person riding a motorbike stopped and requested me to stay at Sapta Matrika Mandir.

Maheswar, situated on the Northern Bank of Narmada, was the capital town of Queen Ahilia Devi. The city is known for its temples and grand Maheswar Ghats. Dutta Mandir, Sankat Mochan Hanuman Mandir, Manteswari Mahadev Mandir, Kashi Vishwanath Mandir and Shri Raj Rajeshwar Mandir are a few renowned temples in Maheswar. Eleven Akhand Jyot (lamps) have been burning from ancient times in Shri Raj Rajeshwar Mandir, built by Sage Parshuram. The mythological story illustrates that Raj Rajeshwar wanted to marry Narmada Mai. Narmada Mai insisted she would marry him if he could stop her flow. He did tapasya for ten thousand years and tried to stop Narmada Mai with his thousand hands. However, he failed to hold her as she passed between thousand hands at Sahastradhara. Later, Raj Rajeshwar during tapasya merged into the idol of Mahadev, and the Temple was named Shri Raj Rajeshwar

Mandir. At the fort was the Ahilia Devi Memorial Complex. The complex is famous for the golden idol of Krishna and a bel pattra (bilwa leaf) tree with three to twelve bel pattra (Aegle Marmelos /wood apple) in a twig.

Swami Narhar Giri Maharaja at Sapta Matrika Mandir was a very soft-spoken, elegant Saint. He interacted with everyone in the Ashram and ensured the welfare of parikramawasis in the best possible manner. He served lunch and dinner to all and then only took his food. In Sapta Matrika Mandir, every morning and evening, satsang was held after puja and aarti. I enjoyed taking part in puja, aarti and satsang.

I went for a darshan of Swamini Shailendra Giri Mai at Tyagi Ashram,. She was in her dhyana (meditation) when I reached the Ashram. Therefore, I sat down and started meditating in the quiet and peaceful environment of the Ashram. After about an hour, she came out, sat for some time, gave me ladoo prasad, and blessed me.

In Maheswar, I asked an enlightened Saint how to eliminate the flashback of samskaras (memories), the root problem of all agitation. He explained the functioning of Mann (conscious mind), Buddhi (intellect), Chitta (subconscious mind), and Ahankar (ego- false knowledge of Self). In a dormant form, the subconscious mind is the storage cabinet of samskaras (memories, likes, dislikes, love, anger, hatred, jealousy, etc.). When samskaras pop up due to actual or imaginary sight, smell, taste, sound, or touch, it turns into vrittis (subconscious thoughts). Under the influence of false knowledge (ego), innermost thoughts (vrittis) throw up positive or negative files from the storage cabinet of the subconscious mind. Generally, the subconscious mind is more powerful and controls the conscious mind. The thoughts get reflected as positive or negative emotions and actions depending on the triggered memory. A feeling, in turn, affects life energy (prana). Positive thoughts calm the prana, whereas negative ones agitate them.

The conscious mind works out solutions for any agitation within us. We are comfortable with our senses; therefore, the intellect automatically reaches outside to find answers through the outer world. Instead of a solution, an additional layer of agitation adds to the subconscious mind. Bhakti or dhyana (meditation) reduces the energy of negative memories. In bhakti, the individual aligns with the Supreme during spiritual discourse, bhajans, mantra chanting, and unselfish work. Then the focus of the mind shifts from the outer world to the inner domain, where buddhi (intellect) enhances and calms down prana. Satsang builds the right knowledge, which helps to differentiate between right and wrong. With the proper knowledge, the ego dissolves, and continuous subconscious thoughts revolve around higher beings.

In dhyana (meditation), an individual needs to move his awareness from the outside world and be consciously aware of their inner Self. Sensing danger, a tortoise withdraws all exposed body parts within its shell. Similarly, when chitta (mind) is without vritti (innermost thoughts, habits) for an extended period, the energy of samskaras gets erased. Right knowledge prevails, discrimination between right and wrong deepens, and the ego gets dissolved, leading to understanding the true Self. On learning the true Self, Purushartha (act by the will of super consciousness) helps the individual transcend to the domain of Atma (consciousness), the arena of the ultimate bliss. As the practice ascends, the reflecting knowledge of the Self also gets dissolved in the Self, and only the Self (consciousness) remains. In short, he explained the entire pathway to self-realisation. It took some time for me to infuse the knowledge within. I felt sanctified and bowed down on his feet. After showering blessings, he instructed me to go to Narmada Mai, pray to her, ask for forgiveness from everyone I may have hurt or offended, and forgive everyone who had knowingly or unknowingly hurt me.

After the discourse, I went to the Bank of Narmada Mai. I did dhyana and forgiveness exercises and sat in stillness and calmness. After that, I went to the Ashram. Around midnight I went to sleep and woke up early morning. During the next few days, a flood of different levels of awareness and perception regarding the Self and society helped me remain happy, blissful, calm, and energetic. I started seeing righteousness in people all around. The level of meditation also deepened. I felt blessed.

After staying in Maheswar for a few days, I walked to Ganga Jhira, Mandleshwar. I was fortunate to be part of the discourse on moksha with a Saint. According to him, an individual can get liberated if he unconditionally surrenders to the Supreme. When Arjuna unconditionally surrendered, Krishna narrated Bhagavad Gita. Sita unconditionally obeyed Ram to walk on fire; she came out without being burnt. It takes a lot to verbalise the realisation/experience by an individual. The Saint narrated a story. An enlightened person whom the King wanted to be Prime Minister left for sanyas (sainthood). The King sent a messenger to the Sanyasi with a request to consider the proposal of the King. On hearing the offer, the Sanyasi looked at a living tortoise and asked the messenger what he would choose if given an option of being a living tortoise or the golden one kept in the palace. The messenger replied, living one. Sanyasi said, "I want to be a living being and not a captured tortoise in the castle". The Saint explained the working of energies within an individual, using a snake as an example. When the power within the snake strengthens, it unfolds from the coil and lifts itself straight without having bones. When energy is released, it recoils itself.

Similarly, the power of kundalini works on an individual. On surrendering the Self to the supreme, strength comes from consciousness. During alignment with the spiritual divinity, the communion with the Divine enhances, and energy flows from Muladhar (Root) Chakra through Swadhisthan (Sacral), Manipur (Solar), Anahat (Heart), Vishudhi (Throat), Ajna (Third-Eye) upto Sahasrara (Crown) Chakra, showering wisdom and bliss.

I asked, "How could ignorance be removed to avoid a misery trap"? He explained - that an inward-looking individual who understands and is aware that the Self, Atma (consciousness), is the source, power, and strength of all knowledge. The desire to experience the Self arises out of Atma. Ego, lust, greed, anger, hatred and jealousy has its roots in false knowledge. Thoughts ignite energy. It is neither right nor wrong; they are just energy. Energy moves through the channel of the current flavour to take action in the waking and dreaming state, depending on our level of ignorance and knowledge. No one gets angry, greedy, arrogant, or jealous in a deep sleep. In a waking state, an individual becomes wild if a desire is unfulfilled. When an individual gets upset, they must go at the source of the anger and try to find out who is angry - Atma, mind, or body? From where is the knowledge of rage coming? An individual is upset in his mind; however, it is just a reflection through others, and the medium is the Self. When an individual desires something and cannot acquire it, he becomes angry. When he sees others having it, jealousy creeps in. Intentions come from within; however, even without verbalising, it starts bearing fruits through others. When results are as anticipated, the desires increase. Below expectations, the impact causes stress, jealousy, and anger.

Thought leads to actions, and intention attracts results. To the western scientist, it is known as the Law of Attraction. Control over the mind and the power of discrimination between right and wrong decreases with negative thoughts and feelings. Under negative emotions, people behave like animals. Therefore, we must channel our energy correctly and not act like animals. He explained this principle with a few examples.

As the Sun provides energy to this world, similarly, our Atma delivers power to us. The universe is a creation of the Divine's energy. Therefore, there is no difference between the Atma's and the Sun's energy. The Divine is the centre point. He is the creator, preserver, protector, and destroyer. Out of ignorance, an individual enters the trap of negative emotions such as anger, jealousy, lust, attachment, terror, and disgust. He shows love, compassion, courage, peace, and tranquillity in gaining knowledge.

Once, King Kaushik visited the Ashram of Saint Vashishta with his entire army. Rishi Vashishta had Kamadhenu, the wish-fulfilling cow. With her help, he was able to feed the army. The King desired the cow, but the Rishi refused to part with Kamadhenu. The King tried to take Kamadhenu by force and lost the war. Kaushik went into tapasya to please Lord Shiva and gain powerful weapons. With new weapons from Lord Shiva, Kaushik challenged Rishi Vashishta but was defeated.

Kaushik again went back to the jungle and started doing tapasya. He was offered the title of Rajarishi Vishwamitra on attaining a certain level of wisdom. Not satisfied, he continued his tapasya. However, Menaka, sent by Indra, could distract Vishwamitra from continuing tapasya, and Shakuntala was born from them. Later Vishwamitra left Menaka and again went into deep tapasya. Indra, this time sent Rambha to divert Vishwamitra, and in anger, he cursed her. Vishwamitra realised that losing his emotional control was out of ignorance. He felt guilty and disappointed. With further tapasya, he could control his emotions and became Jitendriya (power over all the senses and organs). Brahma gave darshan to Vishwamitra and said, "From today onwards, you are Brahmarishi."

Fire in the wood can burn a dead body; however, the same fire also burns the wood into ash. Jealousy, greed, anger between King and Rishi, lust and attachment with Menaka were natural for the King. After tapasya, King Kaushik could shred his ignorance and acquire true knowledge of the Self. He gained full control of his senses with the knowledge and became an enlightened Saint – Brahmarishi Vishwamitra. Similarly, enlightened individuals control their minds and sense organs to continuously transform their negative energy into positive vibrations and bring grace to themselves and their surroundings.

After the discourse, I went for the darshan of Mandleshwar Mahadev, Kashi Vishwanath, Ram Mandir, Dutta Mandir, Eleven Mukhi Hanuman, Shani Mandir, and Gupteshwar Mahadev. Bharti, the wife of Saint Madan Mishra, had left her body for eternal peace in Mandleshwar.

Narmada Mai has a pre-designed path for parikramawasis for their self-realisation. I was experiencing myself, the unfolding of knowledge from the day I took the sankalpa. Blocks got added through discourse, grace, immersion, chanting, meditation, sadachar, and new habits. What a great thing to happen.

In life, everything that goes out, comes back. Knowledge to experience the Self, arises out of the Atma (consciousness), which is the source, power, and strength of all the knowledge. Desire, arrogance, jealousy, greed, hatred and anger have its root in the ego (false wisdom). On surrendering oneself to the Divine, strength and energy come from consciousness. Positive energy clears the negative layers of the conscious and subconscious mind. Unconditional surrendering of the Self to the Divine leads to alignment with spiritual divinity, and energy flows in the right direction, bestowing lasting bliss.

Scriptures of Sanatana Dharma have laid the path for self-liberation with specific steps. The Narmada Parikrama is a laboratory to experiment law of spirituality, the ecstasy of nature, the company of enlightened Saints, Vedic culture, Bharat's glory, and an appropriate path for self-transformation based on an individual's capability. Satsang, spiritual discourses, bhajans, mantra chanting, meditation, and selfless service helps in slowing the prana vayu. Discrimination starts increasing as the pressure of samskara starts going down. Ultimately ego gets dissolved, leading to the unveiling of our true self. In the lap of Narmada Mai, I felt rejuvenated.

OM Peace, Peace, Peace
Narmade Har.

Alignment

A blind girl fell in love with a caring and loving boy, and after a few years of their friendship, the boy proposed to the girl for marriage. The girl said that she would marry if she had a vision and could see from her eyes. After a few months, someone donated a pair of eyes, and the girl got her vision. As she looked at her friend, she realised that he was also blind, and therefore she refused to marry him. The boy felt betrayed and walked out of the relationship. The boy wrote her a letter requesting her to care for his eyes. It shows how the mind changes with changing circumstances, and so do our perceptions. We sometimes fail to appreciate the past because we need to consider the conditions prevailing before the present time.

After darshan and puja at Mandleshwar, I went to Kapil Ashram, Sulgaon. The Ashram is at an elevated place. I took around a hundred steps to reach the Ashram. It has a Temple of Lord Narasimha, two halls, and a cave where Swami Ji does tapasya. He comes out for food in the afternoon and after 9.00 pm. The next day was Holi -the festival of colours. For the occasion, villagers gathered near the Mandir for Holika Dahan (fire worship) at 4.00 am. They did puja of Holika fire and enthusiastically played drums and music. From Sulgaon, I came to Ram Mandir, Pitamali, along the bank of Narmada Mai. The Mandir was in the village, surrounded by houses. After darshan and prasad, I slept for some time. People played Holi with colours. Faces and clothes having different shades of colour were fascinating.

Around 3.00 pm, other parikramawasis and I started walking. We came to Dhareshwar, tapobhumi of Saint Dhareshwar, Sarathi (charioteer) of Lord Krishna. After the darshan of Dharukeshwar Mahadev, I proceeded through a dusty village road to Manokamaneshwar Mahadev Temple, Semrela. This Temple complex on the Narmada bank has two temples, a hall for parikramawasis, living rooms for Sanyasis, and utility areas. After bathing in Narmada Mai, I had a darshan at the Temple. Then I did my meditation, puja and aarti. The village elders had organised a get-together in the Temple complex with an elaborate arrangement of takkar (thick roti with ghee), dal, and sweets. A glimpse of the rich culture and hospitality of the place was evident during the party. We all had dinner around 10.00 pm, followed by a sweet dish.

After completing my rituals the next morning, I visited Mr Bhojpal's house for balbhog. The front room of the house was bigger than a three-bedroom flat in Mumbai. The interior of the hall had eye-catching woodwork. After playing with his kids, I came to Bimleshwar and had a darshan of Bimleshwar and Chandeshwar Mahadev. Chandeshwar Mahadev Mandir has eleven Mahadev Lingas - one in the centre and ten in the outer circles. The Temple bell weighs six moans (roughly 320 kilograms).

From Bimleshwar, I walked up to Kheri Ghat (Nav Ghat). After the darshan of Awaduteshwar Mahadev, I had prasad and lunch at the Virat Kutir Trust Ashram. From Kheri Ghat, I started around 3.00 pm and came to

Charukeshwar Mahadev Complex. The complex has a single vat vriksh (banyan tree) spread across three-four acres. It is known as a Siddha Place (place of spiritual accomplishment). Under the tree, I did meditation and felt blessed. I was sitting on the veranda of the Ashram when a Saint came out of his kutir (room). Seeing him, I stood up, bowed, and said, Narmade Har. His face, filled with Divine grace and an aura full of calmness, had a soothing effect. I wanted to ask him to spell out workable steps to advance in the spiritual life; however, he was internally within himself. Thus I kept quiet. After some time, he asked me, - are you doing parikrama with zeal to know your true Self? On giving a positive expression, the Saint narrated systematic techniques to attain one's goal of lasting bliss.

A human is an individual serving self, and to survive, they need to harmonise relationships with external beings. The long-term benefit of a relationship with ethical and social restraints (yamas) is cheerful. The Law of Karma stresses having compassion for the Self and others and not harming (ahimsa) others for self-gain. Ethical communication is to speak the truth (satya) in the right manner, at the right time, in the right surroundings, and to be neutral to all. Individuals need to exert their rights for a gracious living, refrain from taking what belongs to others (asteya), and have a relationship with the Divine to foster an understanding of our highest Self. That is possible with the abstinence of sexual relations (brahmacharya) and redirecting the sexual energy to the spiritual Self. Divine has provided wealth for general prosperity, which can only be maintained if individuals consume what is needed rather than satisfy their wants. Therefore, acquiring and using what is necessary is essential rather than showing greed and hoarding wealth (aparigraha). According to the ethical codes, an individual can purify themselves, contribute to their surroundings' general happiness, and save wealth for future generations.

The importance of personal observances, moral conduct, and ethical code (niyama) greatly affects ego, belief, thoughts, habits, and actions towards Self and others. An Individual's growth and lasting happiness begin with the purity and cleanliness (saucha) of physical, mental, and emotional beings. Contentment (santosh) comes with reasonable desires and wants. When an individual primarily uses energy to create a union with the Divine (tapa), craving for outward desires loses significance, and they get attracted to healthy food habits, body postures, and optimal breathing. Learning is the basis of human evolution. Being aware of the Self and learning to know thyself for lasting happiness (swadhyaya) helps an individual be centred, be away from non-dualities, and reduce craving for external fulfilment. Knowing "Who am I" is only possible if we unconditionally surrender to the Divine (Isvara pranidhana).

After listening to the sermon from the Saint, I sat silently, trying to internalise the teaching and evaluate myself on the spiritual development scale. I made specific changes in my daily practices based on my newfound awareness. The lessons from the discourse occupied my mind as I walked through the canal route to Warwah town. After the darshan of Nageshwar Mahadev in Warwah, I came to Kalka Mandir. Four parikramawasi, staying in Kalka Mandir, were preparing dinner, and on seeing me, they added a little more rice. After dinner, I washed my clothes, bathed, and all of us slept in the Mandir Hall. In the dream, the entire discourse flashed before my eyes.

The next morning, I woke up early to spend an hour to regain awareness of the structural changes required and reschedule my activities accordingly. Around 6.00 am, we started for Sulgaon.

Toward the outskirts of Warwah town are the training ground and barracks of the MP Armed Police. Just ahead of the police complex, the jungle starts. Soldiers were exercising within the boundary of the complex. Officers were jogging/ walking on the road passing through the forest. I was physically walking but mentally engaged in planning and working out my schedule for self-growth. After nine kilometres, we reached Sulgoan village, the first village on the route.

Since morning a bhakt was waiting for parikramawasis on the outskirt of the village. On seeing us, the bhakt escorted us to the residence for balbhog (breakfast), which we enjoyed. Then, moving ahead through the dirt road of the Lakar Kote Jungle, we came to Kundi. After lunch and rest, we walked further to Hiraniya and then Taranniya. We cooked our food (dal and roti) in a group at night and slept in the Panchayat Bhawan's open courtyard on the Kanad River's bank. Villagers' farms were at the back of the Bhawan, followed by dense forest. Across the river Kanad, rows of trees covering the forest glittered with the reflection of the Moon in the water. After a long gap, we slept without the nuisance of mosquitoes. The weather was pleasant, with the trickling sound of the flowing water of river Kanad. The Glittering Moon, stars, barking dogs, and rows of trees across the river made it an ideal place.

The next morning after crossing the river Kanad through knee-deep water, we came through a dense jungle dirt road to Ram Mandir, Pipari. We visited Sita Kund (water spring) on the outskirts of the village. Narmada Mai is around five kilometres from this place; however, water in the kund flows from the Narmada. Water is filled through a diesel pump in the kund since it has dried up. Next to the kund are Valmiki Ashram and Luv-Kush Cave. One Sage lives in the Valmiki Ashram (small hut). Around two hundred feet above the Valmiki Ashram is the Ram Temple. In the early twentieth century, the King constructed the Ram Temple with the idols of Ram, Sita, Laxman, and Hanuman. He also built a place for the priest and parikramawasis within the complex. He donated two hundred acres of fertile land to ensure that the income generated from the sale would be sufficient to maintain the complex and care for the parikramawasis. Remains of the Temple's outer wall still have a few idols of various deities. The family of the priests stays in the complex. Next to the complex is a huge tree. After darshan, I spent some time under the tree. I then walked along the road to Hanuman Mandir, Bawadi Khera, surrounded by forest.

From the Hanuman Temple to Ratanpur, I walked three kilometres on the village path. Finally, I reached the waterfall and ancient Jayanti Mata Mandir through the forest, full of tall teak trees. Near the waterfall is the cave where Rishis did tapasya. This waterfall never dries up.

The ancient Temple of Goddess Durga has a reference in Ramayana. Mythological stories narrate that the area was tapobhumi of Rishis and Munis. Demons used to harass them. To help the Rishis and Munis, Goddess Durga fought with the demons and defeated them. In remembrance, this Temple is named Jayanti Mata. The importance of this place is also due to its holiness and natural green scenery. This gated Temple has a vast complex with separate idols of Durga Mata, Lord Ram, Sita, and Lakshman. There are a few rooms for priests and a hall for parikramawasis. Wild animals roam near the Temple, and therefore after aarti gates are locked. During Dussehra, more than five thousand people visit this Temple and the waterfall.

Throughout the night, the volunteers were busy cleaning the premises of the Mandir and getting the complex ready to welcome devotees for Dussehra. In the evening, we did aarti and prayer in the Mandir. Parikramawasis had high-class dinner prasad late at night. In the morning, I stayed back at Jayanti Mata Mandir for aarti and continued my journey. Due to the apprehension of an animal attack, parikramawasis are not allowed to stop in the jungle. Midway an idol of Lord Hanuman stands tall, and a rivulet flows nearby. I felt the vibration of peace and tranquillity and bowed in front of the Lord. I covered a distance of twenty-one kilometres through the dense jungle. After crossing the wilderness, I reached Pama Kheri around 1.00 pm and headed for the Ashram near the highway.

Walking alone in the parikrama, especially in the forest, was a life-changing experience. It gave me confidence and a sense of understanding of the vastness and expanse of nature. I started enjoying the silence, got attached to the environment and started admiring minute details I had never observed. Different shades among trees, plants, flowers, insects, butterflies, birds, and animals became interesting. I feared walking alone in isolated areas. However, newly found confidence shredded them. Walking on a rough road acted as a natural acupressure.

Four parikramawasis had arrived at the Ashram around 10.00 am and had prepared lunch. After lunch and rest with other parikramawasis, we walked thirteen kilometres to reach the newly constructed Dharmeshwar

Mahadev Ashram, Pokhar. Pandavas built the original Dharameshwar Mahadev Temple, and Yudhishthira did sthapana (invocation of the Divine), hence the name Dharameshwar. Due to the dam's construction over the Narmada, the original Temple got submerged in Narmada Mai. The new Temple complex is opposite the forest and next to the highway. In the complex is Rewa Kund, filled with Narmada water. The Management of the Temple served dinner and breakfast.

From Pokhar, I came to Fatehgarh. The village is on the bank of sangam of the river Datoni and Narmada Mai. After having lunch with a boatman, I crossed the Datoni River by boat. On the way, I met other Parikramawasis, and I joined them. Before Nemabar, a female parikramawasi moving in a group slowed down due to pain in her leg. After walking a few kilometres, the group stopped and was not eager to proceed. They also pleaded with me to stop. I encouraged them to walk another two kilometres and spend the night in Nemabar since it is a tirtha (an important pilgrimage). On their request, I moved ahead to Nemabar, found out the route to Bhramachari Ashram and waited for other Parikramawasis on the outskirts of the town. Other parikramawasi reached Nemabar around 7.00 pm. We all went to the Bhramachari Ashram, which has the footprints of Vasudev Saraswati. During the day, we covered a distance of forty-one kilometres. After bathing in the evening, we went for aarti, followed by satsang (spiritual discourse). Ghat at Nemabar is grandeur. In the morning, around 4.00 am, I took a bath in Narmada Mai. Early morning also, the place was full of devotees. After the darshan of Siddhanath Mahadev, I came to the Ashram and saw two devotees performing Surya Namaskar (Sun Salutation) on mantras chanted by Swami Ji.

Surya Namaskar, also known as Sun Salutation, is a very important asana in yoga. Indian scriptures have laid down many benefits of yogic postures. Body movement in systematic yogic postures, synchronised with the right food and breathing techniques, ensures good health, flexibility, and stamina enhancement. It also calms the mind and brings structural changes in life within a physical, astral, and casual plane, ensuring alignment within the Self and with external and superior forces.

From Nemabar I came to Panch Mukhi Ram Mandir, Pipalaneria. After meditation and rest at the Mandir, I proceeded to Shree Narmada Ashram, Sealkanth. The next morning after walking for three hours, I came to Chinnda Gaon, had lunch at a bhakt's house, and came to Dimawar. After resting under a tin shed across the road, I started walking and crossed the Timrani River, which had dried up, and through Riau Gaon, reached Mamleshwar Mahadev Mandir, Mandarnapur and spent the night.

Early morning, I saw two devotees practising pranayama (breath work) in the Mandir. Regulation of breath (pranayama) within the body is essential as it optimises vital energy for an individual's performance, maintenance, and relaxation. An individual balances the flow of energy from the base (Muladhara) chakra to the crown (Sahasrara) chakra and purifies the body's subtle nerve channels through pranayama. With slow rhythmic breathing, the energy within all parts of the body balances. The right amount of heat is generated, which melts the blockages of nerves (naris) and redirects the mind within, leading to calm, purified, and focused thoughts.

From Mandarnapur, through the road and along Narmada bank, I reached Saat (seven) Shrotra (sublets). At this point, Narmada Mai flows through seven mini islands. The formation of Saat Shrotra has patches of greenery and rocks through which water flows. It was pleasing to the eyes. Sitting on the bank, I watched the beauty of Narmada Mai. From Aavari Ghat, I walked through fields to cross the Bhagner River. The downhill slope before the Bhagner River was very steep and slippery. I carefully climbed down in a sitting position taking baby steps and reached Narmada Mandir, Holipura.

From Holipura to Budhni, I took Highway SH 22. The road was extremely busy, and the pollution from the trucks was choking my lungs. From Budhni, I walked to Hobapura, an old spiritual town on the bank of Narmada Mai. The place has many temples, and the Ghat on the Narmada bank is magnificent. I spent a night at Ram Mandir. Early in the morning, I went to the Ghat and bathed. I climbed down three floors to reach the river. Many devotees had gathered at the Ghat. After the bath, they performed rituals, a common thing along the Narmada River. From Hobapura, I came to Budhni, an industrial town, couriered my woollen clothes to Mumbai.

Further walking down SH 22, I rested at Hanuman Mandir, Bandra Bhan. After rest, I came to Banita via Jagdish Mandir, Shahjang and spent the night alone on the veranda of Ram Mandir. The next morning I started walking from Banita, and through wet fields and marshy land along Narmada Mai, I reached Hathnora. At this place, Narmada Mai flows in the North direction. From Hathnora to Narayanpur, the road with big potholes made walking difficult. I got tired and therefore took a rest at Narayanpur. By evening, I reached Maa Kripa Dharamshala, Bharchak. This place was the tapobhumi of Saint Bhrigu. From

Bharkach onwards, I walked on the village road / pagdandi, and through Gadar Baas, San Khera, and Motalsar came to Bagalbara. I lost my way a few times and had to walk a few extra kilometres.

Being Ekadashi, the Saint at San Khera offered authentic mattha (buttermilk with spices, sugar and dry fruits), which I enjoyed. I had lunch at Bagalbara, and by afternoon I reached Satravan, where Arjuna had pierced his arrow to fetch water. I came to Motibai Asham at Ghat Piparia for the night's rest. The next morning, I reached Mangarole around 9.00 am. At Jai Shri Ram Ashram, near the bridge, I met Bhaskar Purohit, who requested me to have lunch at his place. Bhaskar was a Sanskrit Scholar at Mahakaleshwar Temple, Ujjain. We had a long and exciting discussion on spirituality, parikrama, and religion.

After lunch and rest, I walked along the banks of Narmada Mai, then through the village and banana plantation to Shri Ram Janki Mandir, Mohar. The Mandir is on a hillock, and behind the Mandir is a jungle. After a long walk, I felt exhausted; however, I bathed, washed my clothes, and relaxed. All parikramawasis' slept on a platform under the open sky next to the flower bed. Around midnight red ants flooded the place, and we all had to shift to the Temple's veranda. On the banks of the Narmada Mai, I got a lot of inspiration and new experiences, which added to my knowledge, love, patience, peace, and confidence.

Early morning at Andia, I had an eye-catching darshan of Ram Janki Mandir, Boras. Within the Temple complex is a renowned Sanskrit Pathshala. Just below the Mandir is Sita Ram Ashram. The continuous singing of Ram Dhun (24*7*365 days) had a powerful impact. From Andia, on my way to Anghora, I was astonished to see a beautiful hatched madhia (Ashram) on the bank of Narmada Mai. I walked into the Ashram to find a different world. The roof thatched with hay, the walls made of bamboo pieces, and the ground covered with bamboo chatai (rug), cushioned with soft grass, was a wonder of its kind and worth experiencing.

The knowledge-packed satsang with Swami Ji in the Madhia on pratyahara and dhyana had flavours of different perspectives. Pratyahara is moving the Self away from external sensual distractions, resisting reactions to external stimulants and returning to spirituality to gain internal peace. Swami Ji conducted a guided meditation for about an hour at my request.

After practising meditation, I came to Shree Swami Samarth Math, Anghora. It is a vast Temple complex on the bank of Narmada Mai. Families had gathered, and couples were doing puja as Swami Ji was chanting mantras. Once the puja was over, everyone had lunch and rest.

In the afternoon, I walked along the river to Saint Ganga Das Ji Samadhi, Shuklapur. Bhakts believes their wish will materialise by doing one hundred eight times parikrama at Saint Ganga Das Ji Samadhi. Saint Ganga Das gave life to a dead bhakt is a popular belief in the area. I saw many people taking parikrama around the Samadhi to ask for the fulfilment of their desire or pay gratitude for fulfilled wishes. Once a year on Guru Purnima, there is a huge gathering of devotees at the Samadhi.

From Shuklapur along Narmada Mai, I came to Ram Mandir, Kadori. Due to the hot weather, walking between 11.00 am and 3.00 pm became difficult. After resting at Ram Mandir, I started for Chattarpur. Beautiful mud houses, courtyards painted with different colours, and ground polished with cow-dung water were common along the route. The village road was very dusty, with plenty of two-wheelers and tractors. Green/ red chillies, cereals (moong), wheat, and vegetables are grown in the area. I had to navigate through dust and wheat farms with hay up to shoulder level. After walking for about thirty kilometres on the dusty path, I got tired when I reached Chattarpur. The house of Damodar Shriwas was the first one in the village. He invited me to spend a night with his family, another timely grace from Narmada Mai. After the bath, I did aarti and puja. At dinner, we had a good time knowing each other. The weather was pleasant, so we all slept in his courtyard under the sky.

I got up at 3.00 am. After completing morning rituals, we left for Barman Ghat, tapobhumi of Lord Brahma. Upto Rukwada, the route was dusty, and after that, I had to walk on an under-construction, uneven, muddy road with a steep climb and a decline. At Rukwada, a passerby told me to leave the road and walk through the village route as I would save seven kilometres. I took the village road and saved a lot of time. Being Purnima (full Moon), many people had gathered at Barman Ghat to take bath and perform rituals for the occasion. The street leading to Narmada Mai had a festive look, with people in colourful clothes and shops selling various kinds of merchandise and eatables.

Barman Ghat has many ancient temples. Ram Janki Mandir and Dharamshala, Dutta Mandir, Radhey Krishna Mandir, Siddha Chintamani Devi, Laxmi Narayan and Someshwar–Dipeswar Mahadev Mandir were the prominent ones. After the darshan of temples, I came to Harihar Ashram, Sapta Dhara. The Ashram is on top of a hill. Narmada Mai flows through a cluster of multi-coloured rocks and many sublets, creating water mists.

The sight is blissful. Being Purnima, many yatris had come to the Ashram, and bhakts prepared varieties of items for lunch prasad. Parikramawasis got room to rest.

A parikramawasi staying in the Ashram joined me. Through the road and pagdandi (village dirt road), we walked to Choti Dhuandhar (small fountain). The sight of the mist was visible from afar, and a close look gave a soothing effect. We crossed several farms and hilly jungle paths to reach Narmada Mandir. During the night, while we were sleeping in the open courtyard, suddenly, there was rainfall with strong wind. It took some time to gather our belongings scattered by the wind.

The route ahead was uneven through the hills. After walking for around five kilometres, I reached Rampura Seva Ashram and celebrated Gudi Padwa, Maharashtrian New Year, with other parikramawasis. All of us relished Puran Poli, a traditional Marathi dish. We climbed on an elevated hillock under a banyan tree surrounded by idols of many Gods/Goddesses and took an afternoon nap. In the afternoon, it started raining. We waited for the rain to stop, but it kept drizzling. A few other parikramawasi joined me, and despite the rainfall, we continued our journey and came to Durga Mandir, Gaushi, to celebrate the first day of Navratri (Durga Puja). One hundred and eight Jayanti (wheat saplings) were sown in bamboo baskets and placed in the hall next to the Temple. The presence of people showed a reunion of family, relatives and villagers. Everyone had come in traditional costumes. The Pratima (idol) decoration with silver lining and the Temple with silver fabric gave a conventional look. As per customs, many weapons placed before the Goddess Durga for her blessings looked amazing.

I asked the priest to narrate the story and relevance of Durga Puja. He said Mother Goddess is worshipped nine nights/ten days during Navaratri (Durga Puja) with great passion and devotion. Goddess Durga is the all-powerful Goddess with the combined power of all the Divine forces. She destroys evil forces and restores peace. The festival celebrates the victory of good over evil. During the festival, people fast, feast, and worship Maa (mother) Durga in a grandeur style and wear traditional costumes.

Goddess Durga has ten arms. All the hands have a symbolic gesture. A conch symbolises the primordial sound OM and the Sudarshan Chakra (discus) centre of creation. Half-bloomed lotus signifies incessant evolvement towards wisdom. The sword represents the sharpness of intellect, and the bow and arrow represent potential and kinetic energy. Trident signifies the three gunas, tamas- inactivity, rajas- activity and desires, and sattva –positivity and purity. Mace indicates a sign of loyalty, love, and devotion. Thunderbolt denotes character, determination, and supreme power; the axe exemplifies the ability to destroy and create. The snake represents Shiva's consciousness and energy, and Abhaya Mudra denotes blessing to all the devotees.

Goddess sits on the lion, the King of all animals. Before the war, Lord Rama worshipped Mother Goddess, the slayer of demons, by offering hundred-eight blue lotuses and lighting hundred-eight lamps. Arms belonging to the family or relatives are placed before Goddess Durga during Navaratri for her blessing.

Goddess Durga's numerous incarnations include Kali, Bhagvati, Bhavani, Ambika, Lalita, Gauri, Kundalini, Java, Meenakshi, and Kamakshi. On all nine days, people worship a different incarnation of the Goddess (also referred to as

Maa) with mantras (words for spiritual transformation), shlokas (holy verses from scriptures), bhajans (devotional songs), offerings, and aarti. The first day starts with Goddess Durga, followed by Goddess Shailputri, Goddess Brahmacharini, Goddess Chandraghanta, Goddess Kushmanda, Goddess Skandamata, Goddess Katyayani, Goddess Kalaratri, Goddess Mahagauri, and Goddess Sidhidatri, respectively.

Devi Bhagawat, Markandeya Puran and Shakti Puran have shlokas (sacred chants) in praise of the Divine interventions of Goddess Durga. Durga Saptashi, a spiritual text having seven hundred shlokas (verses) divided into three parts, narrates the story of the power of the Goddess. King Suratha lost his kingdom to his enemy, and a trader named Samadhi, driven out of his house by his greedy son and wife, came to the Ashram of Medha Rishi (Saint). Even after facing brutal treatment, the King was worried about his subjects' welfare and the trader about his family members. They asked the Saint the reasons for their unnatural worry. Rishi replied that it was due to an illusion (Maya) created by Mahamaya Devi (Mother Durga). Both of them requested the Rishi to apprise them of the story of Mahamaya Devi.

Rishi related the story of the Divine Mother Goddess (Mahamaya Devi). When she appeared, the innate power and weapons came from Lord Vishnu, Brahma, Shiva, Indra and other Gods. She is of Moola Prakriti (root nature) behind all forces in the universe.

During parlay (holocaust), Lord Vishnu was sleeping. From the dirt of his ears were born demons: Madhu and Kaitava. Lord Brahma was sitting on the lotus stem arising from the naval of Lord Vishnu. Both of them wanted to kill Lord Brahma. Lord Brahma prayed to the Goddess Mahamaya (Durga) Devi to wake Lord Vishnu from his sleep. Mahamaya Devi opened Lord Vishnu's eyes. Asuras (demons), Madhu and Kaitava, having tamasic power, were engaged with Lord Vishnu for thousands of years in the war. Lord Vishnu killed both of them.

In the second story, Mahishasura incarnated as a buffalo, defeated Indra and Devas and snatched all their powers. Indra and Devas approached the trinity of Lord Vishnu, Lord Brahma, and Lord Shiva. They came to Goddess Durga to free the world from the demon Mahishasura. She killed Mahishasura and his army.

In the third story, Indra and Devas approached Uma (Goddess Durga) for her help to liberate them from demons Shumbha and Nishumbha. Koushiki / Chandika, incarnate of Goddess Uma, killed Chanda and Munda, the Generals of the Demon Kings. Shumbha and Nishumbha were killed by Goddess Durga herself.

Along with Goddess Durga, people worship Goddess Lakshmi (Goddess of wealth), Goddess Saraswati (Goddess of knowledge and music), Goddess Kali (darker and violent manifestation of Durga), God Ganesh (God of Beginning), and Lord Kartika (God of War). On Vijaya Dashami (the tenth day), the festival ends with the immersion of a clay idol in the water body to symbolise her return to the cosmic Divine.

Medha Rishi said that Goddess had given the boon that anyone who reads or hears her stories shall attain supernatural powers, can fight evil forces and all their desires, and achieve liberation from the cycle of birth and death. After hearing the stories, King Suratha and Trader Samadhi went for tapasya (penance). As per their desire,

King Suratha got his kingdom back, and Samadhi obtained salvation.

At night, guests and parikramawasis had a feast, and we slept in an open courtyard. Puja and aarti continued up to 1.00 am. At night, we woke up, did midnight puja and aarti of Goddess Durga, and felt blessed. However, I experienced a strange phenomenon. I felt overwhelmed as thoughts, words and actions of the past started flowing in a continuum. After that, the flow of gains and struggles of my life, how I overcame them, and the fruits of my action made me aware of some success stories and frightful narratives. An inner voice directed me always to remain mindful of my thoughts and cautiously review self-awareness at regular intervals.

Henceforth, as a routine, I often checked my self-consciousness, remained in the moment, and did an awareness audit every night. This exercise helped me be mindful of the present and twisted the table for blissful living. I felt happy and realised that my evolution continuously demands a different me. It came in increments by knowledge, skills, scars, struggles, and, most importantly, the gift of consciousness. I put in my effort; however, some superior force always helped me. If I have thought or planned something, I have the capability and capacity to achieve it.

At Gaushi, Narmada Mai flows at a distance. We departed from Gaushi and, after walking for a kilometre, took a bath in Narmada Mai and did our morning rituals at the Ghat itself. After Hirapur, we crossed river Harni and came to Harneshwar Mahadev, Jogipura. Here Nandi is shown in a standing position. Standing Nandi is a rare sight in a Shiva Temple. After darshan, I proceeded to

Powal Village, had lunch and slept in an extended gallery of the Mata Mandir.

Yagya and Srimad Bhagawat Katha (discourse) was happening at Barapatti. The mood was festive, and devotees were enjoying spirituality and humility. The episode of Lord Vamana and King Bali was the day's topic. King Bali, even being an Asura, was a devotee of Lord Vishnu. Bali's devotion and noble qualities were intense, and the Lord blessed him. In the war, he defeated Indra and other Gods. He became ruler of the universe and enjoyed all the powers of the Gods. During his rule, everyone was happy, healthy, and peaceful. Agriculture flourished, proper yagya took place, and goodness, compassion, and peace among the subjects prevailed. Distressed, Indra and other Gods sought refuge in Lord Vishnu to defeat King Bali and restore their lost kingdom.

From the womb of Aditi, Lord Vishnu took birth as a dwarf Vamana. King Bali was performing Ashwamedha Yagya. Dwarf Vamana, in the form of a Brahmin singing spiritual verses, came to the yagya. Bali's Guru, Shukracharya, a descendant of Sage Bhrigu, warned him that the dwarf Brahmin was an incarnation of Lord Vishnu, not to offer him anything during the sacrifice ceremony, as he could take away all the wealth of Bali. King Bali replied to his Guru that Lord personally came to his yagya unexpectedly for the welfare of all. He was determined to give anything the Brahmin would ask for in daan (charity). He was ready to undergo any suffering or destruction. Powerful kings have ruled the world, but with time no one remembers them. When approached by a worthy recipient, it is rare that a donor gracefully part with his wealth. If the consequence of charity is poverty and suffering, he was ready to face it.

King Bali, accompanied by the Saints and Brahmins conducting his sacrifice, received and welcomed Vamana and brought him to the sanctum sanctorum of the yagya. Paying respect to the Brahmin, he bowed down. Bali humbly thanked the dwarf Brahmin for abolishing all his sins, purifying his entire lineage by coming to the yagya and making the yagya successful. He further told him to ask for whatsoever he wanted. Disguised as a young Brahmin, Lord Vamana asked King Bali for a piece of land measuring three paces of his feet. King Bali gladly granted Brahmin's wish against the advice of his Guru Shukracharya.

The dwarf Brahmin expanded himself to encompass the whole universe. With His first step, he mapped the Earth, and His second step reached Brahma Loka. Bali offered Him his head for the third step. Later the great bird Garuda tied Bali with Varuna Pasha (noose of Varuna). However, Bali remained steadfast and made the ultimate sacrifice of his ego. Bali told the Lord that getting entangled in wealth would be a sheer waste of his life.

Hearing about Lord Vamana and King Bali, Lord Brahma came to pay respect to Lord Vamana, an incarnation of Lord Vishnu. During the discourse, Lord Vishnu said that when He is pleased with his devotee, he takes away all the wealth from him. With wealth, a person gets obsessed, loses all humility, starts disbelieving others, and forgets Him. After going through numerous lives, a Jiva (consciousness) attains a human form with the Lord's grace. If an individual surrender himself to the Lord, he is not affected by his wealth, lineage, achievements, and knowledge. Surrendering to the Lord is the highest expression of the Divine's grace. Having attained this knowledge, an individual moves the ladder of spiritual advancement. Lord Vamana told Lord Brahma that King Bali had overcome the clutches of Maya, stuck to dharma even in distress, and remained faithful to his vow.

During the next cycle of creation, King Bali will be the God Indra. Lord gave Bali the Kingdom of Sutala to live with his family and subjects. Sutala, handcrafted by Lord Vishwakarma, is difficult to obtain even by the Gods. Lord Vamana returned Indra and the Gods their kingdom, and King Bali went to Sutala with his family and subjects. After the yagya ceremony and Katha (discourse), we went for the bhajan session held in the presence of Shree Devi Das Maharaj. After the sermon, all devotees had dinner and prasad, and I slept. However, post-midnight, strong wind and rain kept us awake.

Early in the morning, I started walking along Narmada Mai. By 11.00 am, I reached Triveni Sangam, Samna Ghat and rested in Parmeshwar Mahadev Temple. In the afternoon, along Narmada bank, I came to tapobhumi of Raja Bali and spent a night at Sita Ram Ghat, Belpathar. After residing for a night, I came to Hanuman Mandir, Ram Ghat. In the afternoon, I proceeded to Gowbhaccha Ghat and by evening, I reached Baba Hari Das Ashram, Saraswati Ghat. The Ashram is on a hillock in a house. Son is a Saint, and family members are his followers. Ramayana has been recited continuously (24*7*365 days) in the Ashram for many years. For the first time, I recited Ramayana for two hours.

From Saraswati Ghat, through the jungle, I came to Ramnagar and walked along the tar road to Tilakwada. At Durga Mandir, a family came to see yagya with two children. Father was driving carelessly; the girl child sitting at the back fell from the tempo and started bleeding. After giving her proper treatment, I continued my journey to Gwari

Ghat, a small town on the banks of the river Narmada Mai near Jabalpur. As per Garuda Puran, performing cremation rites at this place is auspicious. Renowned Rishis and Munis (Saints) have performed tapasya near Siddha Kund. People believe bathing in the Narmada Mai at Gwari Ghat can cure physical ailments. Other important places around Gwori Ghat are Gurudwara of Guru Nanak Sahib, Sai Baba Temple, Jain Temple, and Madan Mahal Rani Durgawati Fort.

I visited the fort after the darshan of Narmada Ji, Mandirs and Gurudwara. After that, I came to Kalidham, a beautiful Mandir of Kali Devi, situated at Kali Ghat. Fortunately, I had a darshan of one thousand eight Akhanda Jyoti (light of burning fire), a sign of victory of good over evil. In the evening, after puja and aarti, I received blessings from Swami Ji. In a short message, he conveyed that an individual is a pure consciousness, veiled by the influence of Maya by manipulation of mind (mann), intellect (buddhi), memory (chitta), ego (ahankar) and jealousy (matsar). The physical body is the Temple where the soul (consciousness) resides. An individual comes to this world to attain the true essence of the truth of absolute being (sat), pure consciousness (chit) and bliss absolute (ananda). He blessed me that during the parikrama, I would realise the true nature of myself. He directed me to go to the Temple and pray to Goddess to lead you from unreal to real (Asato Maa Sat Gamaya), from darkness to light (Tamaso Maa Jyotir Gamaya), and from death to immortality (Mrityor Maa Amritam Gamaya). He instructed me to chant this mantra to delete the poisonous memory I carried in my mind and help me make the right action to drop my ego. Doing this, I would blossom and feel content within, filled with love and radiance. It came as reinforcement of gratifying my dreams of being aware of

"Who am I" and "What am I here for"? I felt blessed, and tears of joy rolled down my cheeks.

Walking alone through jungles, hills, and steep terrain made me fearless and confident, and over time prepared me to approach unknown territories confidently. It allowed me to listen to my inner self and believe in myself. When nobody was there to show the way forward in the jungle and along the rugged path, I just listened to my inner voice to find that I was ninety-five per cent correct. Jungle walking also taught me to concentrate on one thing at a time, walking. While walking, whenever other thoughts came, my mind got distracted, resulting in a fall. Over time, being in myself, focusing on one point, and concentrating on now, taught me the game to move forward despite many hurdles. On every occasion, I showed my gratefulness to Narmada Mai. The flavour of love, compassion and enthusiasm kept me in bliss.

OM Peace, Peace, Peace

Narmade Har.

Expansion

While walking through the fields, I saw butterflies mating. A little further ahead, a bird was flying and getting food for her newborn babies. I narrated what I had seen and asked a Saint about the significance of lust and affection. Lust and attachment are responsible for the universe's creation, existence, and maintenance; however, it is also the root cause of ignorance and false understanding of "I" and "Mine." With affection, we raise children, maintain our family, and preserve our belongings. Parents proudly associate themselves with their kids if a child comes first in class. People spend their life savings on their daughter's wedding. Individuals also resort to unethical practices to satisfy their lust and affection.

From Kali Ghat, I walked under the hot Sun to reach Richai. On the way, a motorist stopped and requested me to stay at his employer's house, Mr Jaiswal, at Richai. On reaching Richai, I went to Mr Jaiswal's house. Mr Jaiswal was observing Navaratri fast and had taken a vow not to speak for nine days. He used to communicate through writing. I was fasting and therefore thought it appropriate to have a darshan of Maa Sharda Mandir, a well-known pilgrimage in the State of Madhya Pradesh.

Sharda Mandir was on a hilltop. It took roughly an hour from the main road to reach the hilltop. The outside temperature was around forty degrees Centigrade. The climb was steep with loose pebbles. Gents, ladies, kids, and families flocked in groups on the street leading to the Mandir. Makeshift shops along the roads did good business by selling food, fruits, and puja items. The Temple was likewise crowded. The Priest helped me come closer to the main door of the Temple. With her blessings, I had a blissful darshan of Sharda Mai and could offer flowers and prasad to her. After staying in the Mandir for some time, I returned and took an afternoon nap at Mr Jaiswal's house.

The entire area from Richai to Amarkantak forms a part of the Maikal range. From Richai, there are two options to go to Amarkantak, either through Mandla or Niwas. After discussions with other parikramawasis and Mr Jaiswal, I decided to go through the Niwas since, along the route, there are ashrams and places to stay. The distance through the Niwas was nearly eighty kilometres shorter.

From Richai, I came to Devari and stayed in Narmada Mandir, managed by Dr Prahlada Patil. My legs had swollen with boils in the sole, and my ankles were paining. After a bath and dinner, I went to Dr Patil for treatment. After the examination, he gave me injections and medicines. In the night, it started raining. I requested other parikramawasis for a place to sleep, and suddenly one of them shouted very rudely. Unpleasant and rude behaviour from a parikramawasi for a small request was neither justified nor acceptable. I kept quiet; however, I got disturbed and could not reconcile for some time. Then, I remembered the discourse - people will create disturbing situations; why should an individual get upset by external sources, opinion, or their views or behaviour?

Turbulence is due to individual behaviour towards

others in the past (knowingly or unknowingly hurting or taking advantage of others) or its reaction to the universe. So I did a forgiveness exercise and went off to sleep peacefully. The following day the concerned parikramawasi came and apologised for his behaviour. It further strengthened my belief - give time for disturbances to settle down, it will also pass. People will realise their mistakes and, if given an appropriate opportunity, will correct themselves. Never stay with a grudge, as it will only harm the Self; instead, forgive, appreciate and pardon them gracefully.

Dindori and Mandla districts have an acute water shortage. It was a common sight along the route – long queues of males, females, and kids, at hand pumps filling water and transporting water jars/containers on cycles and trolleys for daily consumption. Hand pumps or wells are limited, sometimes only one in a village.

From Dewari, we came to Jai Maa Banjari Siddha Peeth, Sakri Ghat. Darshan and meditation at the Temple was a blissful experience. On the way to Bikampur, due to strong winds and heavy rains, we had to take shelter at a shop. We decided to spend the night next to the shop, but could not sleep due to the damp floor, red ants, and mosquitoes. Early morning at 3.30 am, we all walked for a kilometre for our morning ablutions. The village has only one hand pump under a mango tree. After sunrise, there was a long queue to fetch water. After the morning rituals, puja and aarti, we walked to Shahpur and, along the National Highway, crossed two steep hillocks within a dense forest to reach Amer. Mr Jaiswal's family from Mumbai had come to their native village to perform Navaratri yagna at their Kula Devi's (family Goddess) place. They requested us to participate in the yagna and have prasad and lunch. A shamiana (overhead temporary cloth shed) was erected around the yagna to protect people from Sun's rays and heat. With limited air circulation, the temperature inside the shamiana became unbearable. We took shelter under a tree and, after prasad and lunch, slept for half an hour. Around 2.00 pm, through Anakhera, we walked along NH45E to Vikrampur.

In Vikrampur, we slept under the open sky and uneven floor in front of the Hanuman Mandir on the side of the road. The entire area was dry, and people fetched water from far distances. Early morning after bath, we performed puja and aarti, and after that, we started from the Hanuman Mandir along the highway, and by noon we reached Shahpur. Mrs Anita Jaiswal invited us for lunch. A few years back, she lost her eighteen-year-old son due to illness. In his memory, she opened a Dharamshala attached to her residence for parikramawasis. She gave ration, and we prepared batti (Indian bread) and dal. All of us had lunch together. Her hospitality was memorable, with individual care given to all of us.

After lunch, we moved to Jogi Tikaria and slept on the Ghat of Narmada Mai. The weather was cloudy, and in the morning, it started drizzling. After the rain stopped, we walked along the banks of Narmada Mai and came to Dindori. At Dindori, a gentleman seeing us (parikramawasis) hailed "Narmade Har" to us, and we also responded. He works with the Sports Department, Government of Madhya Pradesh. His father wanted to do sewa. Therefore, he built a house on the path of Narmada Parikrama. He or his wife stands on their veranda all day and invites parikramawasis to their residence for tea or food. He offered us balbhog. I preferred roti and vegetables as I had to take medicines;

others had pakora (fried potato) and tea. From Dindori, we walked to Ram Ghat, Dhudhi Ghat, Chandan Ghat, and finally, by evening, reached Bijapore.

As we entered Bijapore, it started raining. On inquiry, we found that the arrangement for parikramawasi's stay is at Shahu Dharamshala. Bijapore is a large village comprising five tolas (clusters of the population) across five kilometres in length. It was already dark, and due to the rain, the dirt village roads and pagans (narrow village roads) were slippery. The path through the village had steep climbs and slopes. All of us had free falls several times. It was pitch dark when we reached the Dharamshala, and the rain had stopped by then. The Dharamshala was next to the road across from Mr Shahu's shop. It had a hall and a small place to cook food. The shop owner provided rice, dal (pulses), dhania, haldi, mirch (spices) and cooking oil. Parikramawasis cooked their food. After dinner, I chatted with Mr Shahu, who narrated his story. He was an ordinary labourer and used to run the family on his daily earnings. He started to take care of parikramawasis, and things changed. He owns five wholesale shops and a few commercial vehicles. He earns around ten times what he spends on parikramawasis.

It rained the entire night. Early in the morning, the winds started blowing. However, the weather was cloudy. As soon as the rain stopped, the hand pump got crowded by the women folk. We had no opportunity to fetch water, so we proceeded without bathing. We freshened up and did puja and aarti on the way. We had lunch and an afternoon nap at Shivala Ghat. We left Shivala Ghat around 4.00 pm, reached Tharpathar late in the evening, had dinner, and stayed the night at the residence of Mahant Shree Shanak Puri Maharaj.

The area is rocky, barren, and undeveloped, with scattered farms of poor villagers. While passing through the Sarwaj village, a poor bhakt invited us for lunch. His mother prepared rice and saag (leafy vegetable) and very pleasingly served us. It was astonishing to see her hospitality which we enjoyed. After lunch, we all slept under a tree on the field dividers. Her daughter was pursuing a course in nursing, and her son worked in a nearby town.

In the evening, as we were approaching Harrie, it started drizzling. There was hardly any traffic on the road. The area looked deserted. The sky was cloudy and dark, the atmosphere windy, indicating rainfall. We were looking for a shelter and a place to spend the night. After walking for around five hundred meters, we saw a gentleman with a lady standing by the road with a bike at the crossing. I leapt forward and enquired about an Ashram or Temple where four of us could stay for the night. At first, he directed us to a Temple. Later, he changed his mind and told us to walk around a kilometre and stay at his house. He was the ex-Sarpanch of the village. At night we got excellent food and a place to sleep. We had to draw water from the well, having a water level around forty-five feet below the ground.

By 4.00 am, we bathed at the village hand pump, did puja and aarti, and started our journey around 5.45 am through the kachi (dirt) jungle path. Morning golden rays of the rising Sun on the dew was sparkling. The smell after the rains was freshening. Houses and trees with a landscape of green hills in the background gave a unique, beautiful, and pleasing sensation. After crossing Harrie through Fari Semehar, we came to Dhamber Village. Amid the jungle is Ram Kutir (hut of a Saint) at Damgarh. Here Narmada Mai is flowing as a tiny rivulet. After preparing our lunch, we had a mediation session followed by lunch and rest. We then proceeded through the dense Amarkantak Jungle, having long saal (teak) trees, dead-leaf carpeted ground, and hilly, uneven rocky paths with all sizes of stones compounded by a steep climb. The beauty of the forest and the mountain range is beyond my comprehension and words. The route was covered with dry leaves and an uneven track with loose stones, pebbles, insects, lizards, and snakes. Very carefully, we moved forward, taking baby steps. As we were about to reach Kapildhara, it started raining. The path became slippery and risky. By the time we came to Kapildhara, I got soaked in rainwater.

At Kapildhara, Rishi (Saint) Kapila had done tapasya. Devotees do have a darshan of the cave where Rishi Kapila did tapasya. Outside the cave is a shed, where devotees take shelter, conduct spiritual pujas and offer food to a Kanya (girl child) and Brahmins. People bathe in the waterfall and proceed to the cave for darshan. At Kapildhara, the water of Narmada Mai flows over a vertical drop of around ninety feet. The river's breadth was about ten feet, divided into three small waterfalls. The sight was delightful. Plenty of monkeys play around and snatch eatables from people. A host of vegetables and herbs grows in this area. It was more of a picnic spot for tourists.

Devotees were engaged in a spiritual discourse with an elderly Saint on 'Dharana', 'Dhyana' and 'Samadhi'. The mind gets internally focused in Dharana, which helps an individual to concentrate for an extended period. Japa of the mantra helps to deepen the meditation on God. By doing so, the individual remains focused, calm and composed. As the meditation deepens, self-enhancement happens; this is called 'Dhyana'. When 'Dhyana' deepens, it leads to Samadhi. Samadhi is of two types – Savikalpa and Nirvikalpa. During Savikalpa Samadhi mind still functions, thoughts and questions arise, and solutions and bliss follow.

In Nirvikalpa Samadhi, the function of the mind dissolves, and samskara loses its influence on the individual. At this stage, with the grace of the Divine and Guru, the seed of samskara gets dissolved, and the individual attains Moksha (very nature of the Self, the supreme state) – oneness with God. In lasting bliss and total freedom, an individual melts his Self or personal identity, assimilates and blends the Self with the object of their innateness. This practice leads to oneness, which is Supreme Cosmic Consciousness beyond the boundaries of time and place.

After darshan and spiritual discourse, we proceeded to Dubdhara, where the Rishi (Saint) Durvasa had done tapasya. The view was spectacular and blissful. It is a unique place for tapasya - the practice of 'Bhakti', 'Dharana', 'Dhyana', and 'Samadhi' and for gaining proper knowledge to unveil the worthlessness of the mundane existence.

From Dubdhara, I proceeded, but other parikramawasis stopped for an evening tea. The road, surrounded by tall green trees and steep and expansive hills, led me to Amarkantak around 7.00 pm. In Amarkantak we stayed at Mritunjaya Ashram. I had swollen legs, low blood pressure, and loose motions. After examination, the Doctor gave me medicines and injections and advised me to get admitted to the hospital the next day. I had saved money from dakshina (donation) received during parikrama to do sewa, kanya bhojan, and facilitate colleague parikramawasis with dhoti, towel, and coconut. Other parikramawasi were in a hurry to proceed. As I had to get admitted to the hospital for treatment, I went to the next-door shop and purchased four coconuts, four sets of dhotis and towels. At night, I told a member, parikramawasi, that I could not walk for two to three days due to my poor health. I did a traditional felicitation of colleague parikramawasis with coconut, dhoti and towel.

The following day, I was escorted to the hospital by two parikramawasis - Ram Das Maharaj and Munna Maharaj. They stayed in the hospital during my treatment. I was given six bottles of saline drip with antibiotics and anti-inflammatory drugs. They refused to go with others saying they would remain with me until I was under treatment. Others also stayed back. After treatment and rest, we walked two kilometres to Mai ki Bagia (garden). In this garden, Mother Narmada Mai came and played. At Mai ki Bagia, we bathed, performed puja, aarti, and exchanged half a bottle of Narmada water with the water from the kund. After that, with the help of the local Saint, we had an elaborate Kanya Bhojan and Bhandara. I decided to stay back for a few days. Ram Das Maharaj and Munna Maharaj also stayed back.

Love and care during parikrama reminded me of the selfless services of my ancestors. My grandfather, uncles and father helped many deserving students complete their studies and get appropriate employment. My grandmother was a pious soul. She sacrificed her food and comfort to help others have a meal and basic comfort. She gave the deprived people her cooked food, bedding and clothes. My mother continues the tradition and distributes clothes, food, medicine and cash to needy people.

Walking through unknown and different terrain - road, pagdandi (dirt road); banana, sugarcane, wheat, cotton, chilli fields; river and rivulets, hills, slopes, and slippery and muddy paths was a delightful experiential learning from nature. It taught me to accept help from whichever source it came from, experts or others. At times the benefit of simple and practical tips can be substantial. Always be attentive and listen carefully, evaluate, and apply any idea if it is feasible, as it may save time and resources. Revisit goals; at times, solutions come from difficult problems.

During problems, I reminded myself, "It shall also pass" ("yeh bhi nahi rahane wala hai"). Parikrama prepared me to achieve higher goals, skillfully adapt myself to the lessons of life, endure pain, and look for solutions. At times I had to take tough decisions for sustenance and overcoming hindrances. It made me move to higher levels. I learnt to enjoy every moment, as the present will never return, and the future is yet to come. Hence concentrate on the "now."

OM Peace, Peace, Peace

Narmade Har.

Reinforcement

Nilesh, a very ethical and disciplined woodcutter, was handpicked by a timber merchant with high pay, incentives, and the right working conditions. He got the best quality sharpened axe. Nilesh was determined to do his best. He always came on time and diligently started cutting logs without wasting time; he used to finish his lunch within fifteen minutes and return to work. During the first week, he cut an average of sixteen trees. His seniors appreciated his efforts. Being motivated, Nilesh tried harder; however, his average dipped to thirteen logs during the second week. A week after that, he tried even harder. However, his productivity kept moving down, and his motivation declined. His colleagues would come and spend time in the machine room to sharpen their axe for about two hours, and after that, they used to cut logs. On average, his colleagues used to cut around fourteen logs a day. Nilesh always thought his colleagues were wasting time in the machine room instead of cutting the trees. Seeing a gradual decline in Nilesh's productivity, his seniors tried to determine the reason for the low results. They found out that Nilesh worked his best and never wasted time. Unable to solve the puzzle, they asked Nilesh the reason for the decline in productivity. Nilesh replied that though he was trying hard every day, he cut fewer and fewer logs. When the last time he had sharpened his axe, his boss asked him. Nilesh got confused and answered, "I have been trying to cut more logs, and therefore, I never had time to sharpen my axe". To be productive, we must regularly sharpen our spiritual, mental, intellectual, emotional, and physical axe. When did you hone your axe last?

Due to the dam on the Narmada River, from Mai ki Bagia, we had to walk along National Highway 45, which passes through the jungle and hills. Munna Maharaja, Ram Das Baba, and I went for darshan of Kabir Chabutara - where Saint Kabir, a renowned Saint, poet, and social reformer, did his tapasya. Kabir Chabutara is a beautiful place in a lush green jungle surrounded by bananas, mangoes, other fruit trees and numerous herbs.

When Saint Kabir was doing penance, there was a water shortage at this place. Pleased by his tapasya (penance), Narmada Mai appeared at this place in the form of a Kunda (small pond), which is full of water till date. In the morning, water overflows in the form of a rivulet. Saint Kabir (Saint of the 15th century AD) composed bhajans in colloquial vernacular for everyone aspiring for spiritual growth, irrespective of religion, creed or caste, and societal status. His bhajans subtly spell out minute aspects of the transcendental, inward, or spiritual journey. He explained the peril and pitfall encountered during the same and the supernatural experiences of Saints. He spent his childhood in a Muslim weaver's family and later became a disciple of Hindu Saint Ramananda.

At Kabir Chabutara, discourse by Saints on the philosophy and writing of Kabir through his bhajan "Nirbhay Nirgun" mesmerised all the listeners.

"Nirbhay Nirgun Gun Re Gaunga Mool Kamal Dradh Aasan Bandhu-Ji; Ulti Pavan Chaddaaunga Nirbhay Nirgun Gun ‖	निर्भयनिर्गुणगुणरेगाऊंगा मूल-कमलदृढ़-आसनबांधूंजी उल्टीपवनचढ़ाऊंगा निर्भयनिर्गुण।।
Man Mamta Ko Thir Kar Laaun-Ji; Pancho Tat Milaaunga Nirbhay Nirgun Gun ‖	मन-ममताकोथिरकरलाऊंजी पांचोंतत्वमिलाऊंगा निर्भयनिर्गुण।।
Ingala Pingala Sukhman Naadi-Ji; Tirveni Pe Nahi Aaunga Nirbhay Nirgun Gun ‖	इंगला-पिंगला-सुखमननाड़ी त्रिवेणीपेहांनहाऊंगा निर्भय-निर्गुण।।
Paanch Pachhison Pakad Mangaon-Ji; Ek Hi Dor Lagaaunga Nirbhay Nirgun Gun ‖	पांच-पचीसोंपकड़मंगाऊं-जी एकहीडोरलगाऊंगा निर्भयनिर्गुण।।
Shunya Shikhar Par Anhad Baje-Ji; Raag Chattis Sunaunga Nirbhay Nirgun Gun ‖	शून्य-शिखरपरअनहदबाजेजी रागछत्तीससुनाऊंगा निर्भयनिर्गुण।।
Kahat Kabir Suno Bhaai Saadho-Ji; Jeet Nishaan Ghumaunga" Nirbhay Nirgun Gun ‖	कहतकबीरासुनोभईसाधोजी जीतनिशानघुराऊंगा। निर्भय-निर्गुण।।

Kabir's philosophy of the Supreme Divine was 'nirbhay' (fearless) and 'nirgun' (without any attributes or virtues). In this bhajan, he has laid down the steps and cautions required during an individual's inward spiritual journey to attain Moksha (the transcendent state achieved as a result of being released from the cycle of rebirth). Fear is the greatest block an individual faces on the spiritual journey. To be fearless, we must defy the law of nature or Maya. The gravitational force of Maya pulls everything down within its space and time. An individual must break Maya's gravity to start his inward journey. He has given the steps to defy the Maya by being fearless (nirbhay) and without attributes (nirgun).

He explains, like a lotus, "I will be seated in tapas/penance". Here lotus represents the flower grown in the muddy waters. To remove the confused state of negativity, I shall be seated in meditation (mind fixed on the Supreme Divine), cutting through the negativity and other forces of the universe. Being in penance of the highest degree, I shall move the life force (prana/breathe) in the opposite direction. Thus, I will raise the energy from the Muladhara (base) Chakra at the bottom of the spine to Sahastradhara (Crown) Chakra at the top of the head.

As the energy moves up, it will defy the gravitational pull cutting across its space. Mind and attachment are the core through which we are pulled towards this world, neglecting the very purpose of our human life of merging the Self with our highest Self. I will control my mind, intellect, harmful tendencies, conversation, and ego and renounce all attachments. Thus, I shall balance and merge all the five elements of the body (ether, air, earth, fire, and water) and transcendent through the space of Maya.

By balancing and merging hot compassionate breath, cold, dispassionate breath, and neutral breath, I shall take a bath in the confluence of past, present, and future combined energy.

I will capture and master all my earthly wishes and align the five kanchukas or sheaths (veils covering the pure consciousness to turn to Jiva) - limiting adjuncts on the individual in respect of space, knowledge, interest, time and authorship – kalaa (limited agency), vidya (limited knowledge), raga (limited desire), kaala (limitation of time), niyati (limitation of cause, space and form); and twenty-five tattvas of Samkhya – purusha, prakriti, mann, buddhi, ahankara; five organs of cognition, five organs of action, five subtle elements, five gross elements, and merge them back into the void space of pure consciousness for the purpose to attain a higher state of being.

On submission at Shunyata Shikhar (emptiness), the Saint, absorbed in oneness with the supreme Divine, will sing thirty-six naad (sound of the first movement within consciousness). From this sound, all the ontological categories arise. The thirty-six categories are - Siva, Shakti, Sadashiva, Ishvara, Suddhavidya, Maya, the five Kanchukas and the twenty tattvas of Samkhya. Established in this state, Kabir asserts that he will move beyond impurity and dualities states and wave the victory flag turning the tide against Maya.

Being completely absorbed in the transcendental realm, I will live in the world of Maya. However, I will still keep the transcendental pure consciousness intact.

After darshan and fascinating discourse, I returned to the highway going towards Kanjaria. In the Kanjaria Reserve Forest, parikramawasis were drinking tea at a vendor's cart. On request, he prepared fresh food for us. We took shelter under the shade of a huge tree, and a Saint from Chitrakoot also joined us. All of us had simple healthy lunch under the tree. After lunch, we slept for around two hours.

At night we stayed in Rai Seva Ashram, Kanjaria. Mr Vinod Rai, a teacher at Government School, runs the Ashram. In his compound, he has an enclosed bungalow for his family, and outside the house, a covered veranda, few rooms, a well-maintained garden, two hand pumps, and toilets for parikramawasis. By the time we reached his place, parikramawasis had occupied the rooms; therefore, we had to sleep on the veranda. After taking a bath, we performed puja and aarti. Parikramawasis prepared food in groups, and we all enjoyed sharing and eating the food. After that, we washed all the utensils and our clothes. The following day after aarti, all parikramawasis left in groups at their convenience.

From Kanjaria onwards, the path was dry and rocky. Through the highway, we came to Durga Mandir, Gorakhpur. The Mandir was closed by the time we reached. Rinku Traders provided us with food ingredients (wheat flour, dal, oil, and spices) and called the Priest to open the Temple. Next to the Temple was a big lake. I fetched water from the lake and cleaned the utensils. Munna Maharaja and Ram Das Baba cooked food, on the wood fire, by the side of the Temple. A few yatris (devotees) also joined in. After lunch, Munna Maharaja and I washed all the utensils and kept them in the appropriate place.

After resting, we continued our journey around 4.00 pm. By evening, we reached Mohtara. At the request of Mr Shambhu Prasad Tiwary, a priest by profession, we stayed in his house. We bathed at the village hand pump, washed our clothes, and rested in the small courtyard before his house. His wife prepared dinner, and all the male members of the family also had dinner with us. After dinner, we slept on the terrace because the courtyard was full of mosquitoes.

Further to Mohtara, due to water scarcity and scattered plantations, the area seemed barren, and poverty among the population was evident. The hot weather became intolerable even in the morning, and walking along the highway became difficult. In the afternoon, we were fortunate to rest under a mango tree by the side of the road. At around 4.00 pm, we left, and by evening we reached Sharda Mandir, Kunda. After bathing, we meditated, performed puja and aarti and cooked food. We went for darshan at Mahavir Mandir the following day and proceeded to Ram Mandir Ashram, Dindori. After having lunch and rest at the Mandir, we started our journey and reached Imlai Rayat around 6.00 pm. Mr Bhaya Lal Pusham requested that we stay with him. So we rolled out our mats in front of his house and rested for an hour. After that, we went to take a bath and wash our clothes at the village hand pump, around 400 meters down the road. After taking a bath, all of us performed puja and aarti. People from the village and family members visited us, and we chatted for some time. After dinner, we slept peacefully.

The following day around 5.00 am, we started walking along NH 543D, and through the dense jungle and hilly ghats en-route Saka, we reached Harra Tola. After lunch and rest, we moved further, and by evening, we came to Chabi and stayed at a bhakt's house. From Chabi, we came to Devgaon, sangam of Narmada and Budner (Burhi) rivers. Devgaon was tapobhumi of Parshuram and Jagadambi Muni. We spent the night at Maa Rewa Prasad Prakalp, Devgaon Sangam. The entire area was dry, passed through hilly slopes, had scattered trees, and dispersed habitation. The weather was dry, with the temperature soaring around forty degrees Celsius. Water scarcity made our journey challenging. Nevertheless, the zeal of parikrama kept us going.

From Devgaon, we took the jungle road to Bilgaon and felt lucky to have a blissful darshan at Shiva and Hanuman Temple. Around 11.00 am, we reached Ramnagar, an old capital city of Gaund, with a palace, a museum and a beautiful Narmada Mandir. All of us spent the entire afternoon in the Mandir. After that, we visited the Shiva Mandir, Madhupuri and spent a night at the

Mandir. The following day, we walked to Suraj Kund and had the darshan of Lord Shiva, Lord Hanuman and Maa Durga. After spending a few peaceful hours at the Mandir, we started walking along the canal, and by late afternoon we reached Maharajpur. Opposite Maharajpur on the Northern Bank of Narmada Mai is Mandla City. The view of the magnificent Mandla Ghats spread in a semicircle was beautiful. The election for the Lok Sabha was on that day, and the police personnel were at all locations. The Caretaker of Maa Rewa Prasad Prakalp at Synan Ghat, Maharajpur, was kind enough to accommodate us for the afternoon. At our request, the daughter of the caretaker cooked dal khichdi for us, which we ate after taking a bath in Narmada Mai.

After lunch and rest, we proceeded to Devbappa Dhanalakshmi Sumanmata Ashram, Shahastra Dhara. The entire area was lush green. Narmada Mai moves in multiple streams through rocky boulders. Due to the Bargi Dam on Narmada Mai, parikramawasis could not walk along the river bank, so we took the road. The next day, we started around 5.30 am, walked eight kilometres in the dense forest and again came to a dry, barren area. After 11.00 am, it became challenging to walk due to the hot climate. We had finished our water. All of us were thirsty, and there was no hand pump within sight to fetch water. We spotted a few mango trees in front of a house along the road. Residents of the houses were resting in their homes with the room air coolers on.

After taking permission from the family, we rested outside the courtyard under the shade of a tree. We started around 4.00 pm when the weather became bearable. After we had walked for an hour, we spotted a hand pump by the side of the road under a mango tree. We filled our kamandals (containers) at the hand pump, washed our hands and feet, drank water, and picked up a few mangoes. By evening we reached Ganesh Mandir, Partan. The Mandir is along the road, in front of the playground, surrounded by residential houses and a few shops. Shopkeepers provided the raw material for dinner, and we jointly prepared batti (thick chapatti) and mango curry. Due to urgent work, Munna Maharaja and Ram Das Baba left for Jabalpur by bus.

From Partan, I walked to Pouri along the road. Beyond Pouri, I entered a dense forest and walked for a few hours to reach Dalka. When I came to the village, it was noon and extremely hot. Alongside the road, Dalka Gramin School was closed, and no soul was nearby. I was feeling thirsty and hungry. Seeing the hand pump, I entered the school to drink water and saw an Adivasi girl filling water in her pot. I was surprised to see the girl because the hand pump was visible from the road, and no one was there. In the vicinity of the school, I could not locate any habitation. On seeing me, she, in a very polite tone, inquired whether I had lunch. I said 'no', and she offered to prepare lunch for me. She showed me a veranda facing east where Sun rays would not come and told me to rest. After about an hour, she came with cooked rice and dal. Lunch was very delicious.

Despite the soaring heat, I slept for three hours. When I woke up, I saw few dogs sleeping beside me. Narmada Mai has her ways of taking care of her devotees. Around 4.00 pm, I started walking and reached Beshua around 6.30 pm. In Beshua, I stayed in Radhey Krishna Mandir. The Pujari of the Mandir was kind enough to provide dinner. After walking for two hours the following day, a Pan Shop owner at Gorakhpur offered balbhog (breakfast). After that, on villagers' advice, I took a shortcut and walked through a field to reach Devari and saved travelling around seven extra kilometres. I stopped at Banjari Mata Ashram, Kalkuhi Ghat, for darshan, lunch, and rest. After a short nap, I started around 4.00 pm from Kalkuhi and reached Bargi dam in the evening.

On reaching Bargi Colony, I went to the Avanti Bai Sagar Dam (Bargi Dam) bank to offer prayers and have darshan of Narmada Mai. Bargi Dam's height is four hundred twenty-two meters. Due to the sunset, the reflection of the golden rays on the pool of water was a splendid view. After sunset, I visited Ganesh Mandir in Bargi Colony, a township made during the dam's construction for the employees. The Temple complex is on the foothills. In the evening, people came for darshan and aarti. After the aarti, they sat for long hours on the benches discussing politics.

The next morning through the jungle road, I came to Bargi. Sun's early morning rays. Birds chirping along the zigzag road through hills was an enjoyable experience. At the crossing of the highway, there were many shops serving snacks. Since I had to walk through the jungle for twenty-five kilometres, I decided to have a heavy breakfast. I went to a vegetarian dhaba (roadside motel), and it was getting cleaned after a busy night (the restaurant had closed at 2.00 am). I ordered curd, which was of excellent quality. After that, I asked the owner if I could get some snacks. He sent his servant to get some hot snacks and fruits. In the meantime, we started discussing parikrama. After eating the snacks, he gave me a detailed map of a road through the jungle, which would save time and take me through a clean, non-polluted area. I offered to pay for the snacks, which he declined to accept.

The market had opened by 9.00 am. I purchased fruits and, through the jungle road, came to Hanuman Mandir, Ghat Piparia. The journey from Bargi to Ghat Pipariya was very pleasant. The route moves through steep curves, ascents, and descents of hills, and lush green trees, with hardly any traffic. Occasionally I heard the sound of a car or a bike. While walking, I went into a meditative mood and did not realise the time and effort required to walk sixteen kilometres. At Hanuman Mandir, I enjoyed my lunch and the afternoon sleep. Around 8.00 pm, I reached Siddheswar Shiva Mandir, Nunpur, through Bichuha Trigada. I rested in Nunpur, and early morning, I walked for seven kilometres by road and then for five kilometres through a dirt road to reach Chargoan. At Chargoan, a bhakt took me to his house and provided a sumptuous lunch and a cool place for an afternoon nap. After lunch and a nap, I visited Shiva Mandir, Mulgai and spent the night at the Mandir.

At Sakal Ghat, I met Mr Rishi Mishra, owner of a small tea shop. He offered me lunch, which had come for him from his house. Instead of lunch, he ate snacks and samosa with tea. He also provided me with a place to take an afternoon nap since the temperature outside was forty-plus degrees Celsius. Around 4.00 pm, he showed me a short route to Mahadev Piparia along the canal. The area was very fertile; however, people were lazy. I talked to a Saint, and he told me that people get their daily food due to government subsidies and therefore do not see a purpose to work. If individuals get their needs fulfilled easily, they stop doing work, which in the long run, develops inertia. Late at night, I met Dr Sanjeev Gheghlot, a Heart Surgeon practising in Narsinghpur.

During the last few days, help came from the least

expected corners. Around Narmada Mai, people do their best to serve parikramawasis, at times much more than their means, without any expectations. I committed to completing the parikrama by a specific date. However, the climatic condition and temperature during the day, usually around forty-plus degrees during the afternoon, did not permit me to walk after 10.00 am and before 4.00 pm. I tried walking upto 11.00 am, and it started taking a toll on my health. My attention shifted from inside happiness to outside commitment, and I started worrying about others' opinions. The schedule got compressed, and that caused stress. With stress, I stopped enjoying the present; my focus shifted to the future. I started having a negative internal dialogue; my confidence decreased, and my fear of not finishing the parikrama on time made me uncomfortable. To complete the parikrama on time, I tried to walk extra in the afternoon, which seized my happiness and affected my health.

From Pipariya, I walked to Bamhori Ghat and took an afternoon nap. After walking three kilometres in the afternoon, I saw a multi-coloured rock formation with multiple layers at Siddha Harthia Ghat, Samnapur. Just above the Ghat was a small hut of Hathia Baba. The place had no electricity and lacked even the basic necessary facilities. I decided to stay at Siddha Harthia Ghat. Baba (Saint) and I bathed in Narmada Mai in the evening. Walking through the rocks was quite rigorous. By sunset, we finished our rituals at the Ghat. Baba was used to the path and helped me climb back to the hut. We rolled out our mats outside the shelter under the open sky.

It was a full moon night, and the Moon's reflection on the river was wonderful. On the west of the hut, we could see farms; on the east, trees were shining over the hills. The whispering sound of flowing water was melodious. After dinner, we had satsang on various topics. I narrated my inner conflict to Baba. He carefully listened to my story and advised me not to worry. He said, by the grace of Narmada Mai, calmness would prevail. I slept well. In the morning, I felt Narmada Mai had shredded all my worries and instructed me to focus on the parikrama. My inner voice was clear and loud; the required help would come at the appropriate time. Early morning after bath and puja, Baba accompanied me a long way to show me a shortcut to Shagun Ghat.

Through Pipraha and Shagun Ghat, I reached Narmada Sangam, Guari Ghat. After lunch and rest, I walked along the bank of Narmada and, for the night, halted at Rani Durgawati Mandir, Choti Barman. The next morning around 5.00 am, I started and walked through Linga Ghat to Narmada Mandir, Pithora Ghat. In the Mandir complex, there were rooms meant for parikramawasis. Food was served to all parikramawasis by Ramesh Kumar, a retired teacher. His house was located across the Mandir and was very spacious, with a traditional architectural design, and well-maintained. His family members served me hot chapattis, dal, and vegetables. After lunch, I slept for about an hour, meditated, and started my journey. In the evening, I reached Rajrajeswari Dham, Tharairi, where the Saints discussed Lord's blessing through good and bad moments.

An individual is capable of reaching new heights of happiness and bliss. No one has a perfect life, nor will anyone have one. Everyone has to go through moments of good and bad times. There is no need to be discouraged from failures, as every failure has a lesson to learn and a door to success. Individuals can always learn from failures, draw their inner strength and bounce back. Circumstances that individuals go through, failure or success, help them build the capacity to attain greater heights in times to come. Accept that everything has happened for a reason and has a useful hidden message.

Something seen as bad can change into something beautiful and inspiring. Please avoid getting stuck with things we have been used to. The next level of life will require a change in lifestyle and a different self. An individual can be aware of the Self by applying appropriate ethical efforts. Over time, the golden blessings of the Divine will flow. Learn from the achievements and failures of people who have acquired great spiritual achievements like Saint Valmiki. Reflect on examples of motivation coming from enlightened people like Lord Buddha, who helped individuals build the capability to get through anything life may offer.

The following day, alongside the bank of Narmada Mai, through Bhatera and Rodhawar, I came to Ganeshpuri Ashram, Ganeshpuri Ghat. In the Ashram, Saints performed dhoni tapasya (deep meditation before the fire) in the afternoon. The Saint was surrounded by eleven stacks of cow dung fire in an open courtyard chanting mantras. The Ashram has a charming Lord Ganesh idol at the base of a peepal tree. Many people came to visit Swami Ji. Generally, people sought his blessings. However, few sought advice to solve their problems. A family having a blind child also called on him. The child kept the entire audience spellbound by singing the episode of the arrival of Lord Rama in Janakpur and Sita Viwah (marriage).

I asked one of the Saints how spirituality serves the

community. He replied Maya (illusion), mithiya (false belief), and nidana (chasing worldly pleasures and longing for fame) are major causes of failure and hindrance to the path of understanding correctness or the right view. From ancient times, the sustenance of the world has been through dharma. Every religion has many facets, metaphysical and the concept of the Divine; ways of liberation from the wheels of birth and death; ethical behaviour, self-restraints, ahimsa (respect for all beings and avoidance of violence towards others), social discipline, rituals, and rules for governing institutions. Dharma is the science and art of living to lead an active life with uprightness, austerity, charity, and ahimsa. Based on the pillar of ethical practices, a highly evolved social structure flourishes. It restrains society from abandoning dharma under ego, sensual desires, hatred, anger, fear, greed, and jealousy and helps individuals walk a purposeful life. It validates and rewards self and social restraints.

I further enquired how individuals with immoral behaviour and excellent network, excel. In contrast, people with ethical behaviour faces resistance and struggles to get their dues. He smilingly said, "Immoral behaviour might seem to pay rich dividends in the short term, but it is an illusion, as sensual pleasure only gives momentary happiness. Immoral behaviour leads to ignorance and delusion. Moral conduct is a key to spiritual growth and lasting happiness. Ethical people emphasise compassion, justice and equality and take moral conduct as a responsibility towards the Self and the world. The interplay between their physical action and subtle energy brings happiness. Everything that goes out comes back again. Mortification of memory, tendencies and ego of immoral behaviour leads to ego, lust, anger, greed, anger, attachment, fear, worry, hatred and jealousy. Thus, over time, unethical behaviour is responsible for the downfall of an individual, with adverse consequences of the same in the present and many future lives. On the other hand, ethical behaviour leads to faith, devotion, wisdom and absolute bliss. With renewed positive subtle energies, an individual has the strength to overcome all obstacles and move on the path of self-realisation.

Diti asked her husband, Sage Kashyapa, to make love to her during the pradosh (the first part of the evening-night twilight period). The pradosh period is a forbidden time for sexual acts, as per Hindu shastra. Sage Kashyapa was unable to convince Diti not to make love during the pradosh period; however, with persistence from his wife, he made love. He later told Diti that she would give birth to two cruel sons who would cause a lot of misery to the world. Diti gave birth to two sons, Hiranyaksha and Hiranyakashipu, born as asuras (demons). Hiranyaksha and Hiranyakashipu in their previous life were Jaya and Vijay, respectively, gatekeepers of Lord Vishnu, whom a Brahmin cursed to take birth on the earth.

Hiranyaksha and Hiranyakshipu were evil-minded, caused destruction everywhere, and troubled everyone. In a war, Hiranyaksha got killed by the Varaha Avatar of Lord Vishnu. After the death of his brother, Hiranyakashipu wanted to defeat the devatas. To gain the blessings of the Lord, he went for penance. During Hiranyakashipu's penance, God Indra and other devatas attacked his kingdom. Lord Indra defeated the asuras and captured Hiranyakashipu's wife, Kayadhu. Seeing that Indra had captured Kayadhu, Narada Muni stopped him from taking an innocent and helpless woman as a prisoner since she had no role in the war. On being released, Kayadhu informed Narada Muni about her pregnancy and had no place to live.

Therefore, she requested Narada Muni to allow her to live in his Ashram and serve him as his daughter. Narada Muni accepted, and Kayadhu started living in Ashram. Narada Muni used to narrate stories about Lord Vishnu to Kayadhu. Listening to the Narada Muni, she developed spiritual bonding with Lord Vishnu. Kayadhu's unborn child (Hiranyakashipu's son Prahlada) received transcendental instructions from Saint Narada. Due to his upbringing in the Ashram of Saint Narada, Prahlada became a devoted follower of Lord Vishnu.

Being pleased by Hiranyakashipu's penance, Lord Brahma granted him a boon that no God, man or animal created by him could kill him, during day or night, either in heaven or on earth, with a weapon, inside or outside his house. On receiving the boon, Hiranyakashipu returned to his kingdom. He found his wife and son Prahlada on earth and returned them to his kingdom.

Being saddened by the death of his brother Hiranyaksha and the condition of his kingdom, Hiranyakashipu decided to take revenge on the Gods (Devatas). From childhood, Prahlada, son of Hiranyakashipu, was a committed devotee of Lord Vishnu. Hiranyakashipu was surprised and furious to hear Prahlada sing Lord Vishnu's praises, and over time his anger became intense. Unable to digest his son's behaviour, Hiranyakashipu asked his guards to kill him. Guards tried their best to kill Prahlada, but he remained unharmed. After that, Hiranyakashipu decided to kill Prahlada himself. He dragged and mocked Prahlada and asked if Lord Vishnu was in the pillar next to him. Prahlada replied softly but affirmatively that Lord Vishnu was indeed there. King Hiranyakashipu went into a rage and knocked the pillar.

Lord Vishnu appeared from the pillar as half man and half lion. In a ferocious voice, he announced that he was Lord Narasimha, an avatar of Lord Vishnu. Then, he dragged Hiranyakashipu to the threshold of his door, which was neither inside nor outside the house. After that, the Lord placed Hiranyakashipu on his lap and killed him with his claws at twilight. Prahlada prayed to God and thanked him for saving him. The Lord told Prahlada to ask for a boon. He replied that a boon would only tie him to the circle of birth and death. So he is and will be happy to live only as Lord Vishnu's devotee. Lord Vishnu made Prahlada the King of Hiranyakashipu's empire. Prahlada ruled the kingdom with love, peace, compassion and equality. During Prahlada's rule, the asuras gave up their evil behaviour and became ethical, peaceful and harmonious. The story is a clear example of how walking on the right path destroys Maya (illusion), mithyātva (false belief), and nidana (chasing worldly pleasures and longing for fame), and it also confirms the attainment of the highest bliss and freedom.

At the request of Swami Ji, I spent a few nights with him. I slept in an open courtyard alongside Swami Ji. He takes a glass of milk for his dinner, meditates through midnight, sleeps for four hours, and wakes up by 4.00 am.

From Ganeshpuri Ashram, walking along the Narmada Mai, I came to Ram Janki Mandir, Pitras. I had a darshan of Swami Sita Ram Das. In the past, Swami Ji had a flourishing infrastructure business and was an expert in dam construction. He has a son who was an entrepreneur and a daughter who was a CEO of an IT company when he took sanyas. After his wife's death, Swami Ji became a Sanyasi and has not been in touch with his family for the last twenty years. During my stay, he narrated many stories from the scriptures. The Mandir had a lot of positive vibrations, and I was blissful doing dhyana, puja, and aarti. After balbhog, we sat for satsang. In the afternoon, villagers gathered in the Mandir and stayed till aarti and puja. He had returned from Hyderabad and had brought fresh mangoes. He prepared dinner for both of us and served fresh mango juice. While having juice, he told me that his son was very fond of mango juice. After dinner, we sat for dhyana and, after that, slept. I left Pitras the following morning around 5.00 am, and along Narmada Mai en route, Khariti and Nemavar came to Dudhi Sangam (confluence of rivers - Dudhi and Narmada).

After crossing the Sangam, I proceeded to Veer Bhadra Mandir, Khera Ghat and had lunch and afternoon rest. I left around 4.00 pm and reached Sandia late in the evening. The next day, I came to Namami Devi Narmada Ashram, Galcha and had the darshan of the Goddess. In the afternoon, I proceeded to Reva Mohari. It started raining by the time I reached Mohari. Mr Kailash Patil's house is on the road. He invited me to spend a night with his family. Two years back, he was exposed to a major electric shock from a high-tension wire, making him immobile. After dinner, I gave massage and pressure points to Mr Patil. He had severe gastric problems, which reduced considerably after the treatment. The entire night we could not sleep due to the heavy rains. Due to wet and slippery roads the next morning, I could not walk to the hand pump. After the rain stopped, I walked along the Narmada River to Rewa Mahar. After that took a village road, and through Isharpur, Papli, and Ramnagar, I reached Shri Paramhansa Ashram, Satwasa. I walked around eight kilometres in the afternoon and spent the night at Panchwati Ashram, Mora Gaon.

Panchwati Ashram had a blissful aura. I met a few Saints staying in the Ashram. Out of curiosity, I asked about the importance of prostration in front of spiritual powers and elders. I realised that prostration before a greater spiritual power helps lower, submit and relinquish the individual ego. The ego is the illusionary wall preventing an individual from understanding the true Self. "Who am I?" The Self is the Divine, Universal Soul or Atama and is free, whereas the ego is illusionary, limited by time, space and the force of nature. Surprisingly, a Saint blessed me and told me I would soon receive the answer to my quest. After dinner, I did meditation and went to sleep. In the dream, I saw a Saint answering my inquiry, "Who am I?"

The following day, I walked through the road to Badwara and Ganera village and took the canal route to Gow Ghat. By afternoon I covered a distance of eighteen kilometres to reach Durga Mandir, Kherapati Dham. It became very hot, and I was unable to walk. Therefore I decided to take a rest in Durga Mandir. In the afternoon, I started for Sanga Khera Kala. However, I took the wrong road and reached Sanga Khera Kala late evening. A devotee asked me to stay at his house; however, my instinct directed me to proceed since the Saints were waiting for me. I thought twice. However, the inner voice prevailed, and I moved to Ram Janki Mandir. At the Mandir, the Saints were discussing the works of Adi Sa⊙karacharya. In search of a Guru, Shankara met Saint Govinda Bhagavatpada on the banks of the river Narmada. Saint Govinda Bhagavatpada enquired from Adi Shankaracharya, "Who are You?" Shankaracharya replied in a devotional composition of six verses known as "Atmashatakam or Nirvanashatkam," a true reflection of the Atma (consciousness), which governs our mind, body, relationship, and the cosmic.

Dawn of Reality | 177

"Manobuddhi yahaṅkāracittānināhaṃ	मनोबुद्ध्यहङ्कार चित्तानि नाहं
Na ca śrotrajihvena ca ghrāṇanetre	न च श्रोत्रजिह्वे न च घ्राणनेत्रे ।
Na ca vyomabhūmirnatejonavāyuḥ	न च व्योम भूमिर्न तेजो न वायुः
Cidānandarūpaḥśivo'haṃśivo'ham	चिदानन्दरूपः शिवोऽहम् शिवोऽहम् ॥१॥
Na ca prāṇasañjñonavaipañcavāyuḥ	न च प्राणसंज्ञो न वै पञ्चवायुः
Na vāsaptadhāturnavāpañcakośaḥ	न वा सप्तधातुः न वा पञ्चकोशः ।
Na vākpāṇipādaunacopasthapāyu	न वाक्पाणिपादं न चोपस्थपायु
Cidānandarūpaḥśivo'haṃśivo'ham	चिदानन्दरूपः शिवोऽहम् शिवोऽहम् ॥२॥
Na me dveṣarāgauna me lobhamohau	न मे द्वेषरागौ न मे लोभमोहौ
Madonaiva me naivamātsaryabhāvaḥ	मदो नैव मे नैव मात्सर्यभावः ।
Na dharmonacārthonakāmonamokṣaḥ	न धर्मो न चार्थो न कामो न मोक्षः
Cidānandarūpaḥśivo'haṃśivo'ham	चिदानन्दरूपः शिवोऽहम् शिवोऽहम् ॥३॥
Na ṇyaṃnapāpaṃnasaukhyaṃnaduḥkham	न पुण्यं न पापं न सौख्यं न दुःखं
Na mantronatīrthaṃnavedānayajña	न मन्त्रो न तीर्थं न वेदा न यज्ञाः ।
Ahaṃbhojanaṃnaivabhojyaṃnabhoktā	अहं भोजनं नैव भोज्यं न भोक्ता
Cidānandarūpaḥśivo'haṃśivo'ham	चिदानन्दरूपः शिवोऽहम् शिवोऽहम् ॥४॥
Na me mṛtyuśaṅkāna me jātibhedaḥ	न मृत्युर्न शङ्का न मे जातिभेदः
Pitānaiva me naivamātānajanmaḥ	पिता नैव मे नैव माता न जन्मः ।
Na bandhurnamitraṃgururnaivaśiṣyaḥ	न बन्धुर्न मित्रं गुरुर्नैव शिष्यं
Cidānandarūpaḥśivo'haṃśivo'ham	चिदानन्दरूपः शिवोऽहम् शिवोऽहम् ॥५॥
Ahaṃnirvikalponirākārarūpo	अहं निर्विकल्पो निराकाररूपो
Vibhutvāca sarvatrasarvendriyāṇaṃ	विभुत्वाच्च सर्वत्र सर्वेन्द्रियाणाम् ।
Sada me samatvaṃ na muktir na bandhaḥ	न चासङ्गतं नैव मुक्तिर्न मेयः
Cidānandarūpaḥśivo'haṃśivo'ham"	चिदानन्दरूपः शिवोऽहम् शिवोऽहम् ॥६॥

Our mind, body, feelings, relationship, wealth, and fame are relative and changing, not the ultimate truth. Nirva⊚ashatakam has a glimpse of the non-changing, formless, timeless, spaceless all-pervading truth. Saints value it as the basic and essential contemplation of the true Self that leads to self-realisation. I have tried to summarise the teachings given by the Saints.

The theme of this holy work rests on rejections and assertions leading to self-realisation.

The rejection are:

I am not the mind, intelligence, ego, thoughts, form or higher being. I do not have ears, tongue, nose, or eyes. I am not the earth, sky, air, or fire.

Neither am I the essential air that everyone breathes, nor the five types of air (Prana, Apana, Vyana, Sudan, and Saman), nor the seven elements (marrow, bone, fat, flesh, blood, inner skin, outer skin). Nor am I the five covering of the body (anatomical structure, physiological structure, mind, intelligence, and bliss) or the five organs of action (speech, hands, feet, reproductive system, and anus).

I have no likes, dislikes, delusions, or pride, nor do I indulge in enmity, friendship, vigour, or competition, nor do I need the four necessities of life (dharma, wealth, desire, and liberation).

I am not attached to good deeds, sins, pleasure, or sorrow, nor do I have requirements of a tirtha, holy water, holy books, or fire sacrifice. I am neither the food nor the consumer of food.

I am not fearful of death, nor do I differentiate by caste. I do not have a father or mother, relations, friends, Guru, or students because I was never born.

The assertions are:

I am free of thoughts, beyond imagination or form, all-pervading, and everywhere. I am the regulator of sense organs, impartial to everything and everyone. There is no bongade or liberation for me. I am Shiva, Auspiciousness, Joyful Supreme Being, Consciousness, Emblem of Truth, Nature of Knowledge, and Eternal Bliss.

This devotional work of Adi Shankaracharya opens all the doors of knowledge and wisdom required by a devotee on the path of self-realisation and liberation. I meditated on the meaning of Shankaracharya's work. I was delighted to have initial awareness of the sense of my quest "Who am I?" from the teachings and exceptional experiences during the parikrama.

The following day, I assimilated the learnings and started early. I walked for around two hours without knowing the time until I arrived on the bank of Tawa River. After crossing the river, I arrived at Bandravan. After that, I proceeded to Sethani Ghat, Hosangabad. By noon I reached Nageshwar Mandir, took a bath in Narmada Mai and being Ekadashi (eleventh night of Moon) day, I felt blessed to have prasad at the Mandir. There were lots of Sadhus (Saints) and bhakts who had gathered at the complex. "Society is crumbling" was the discussion of the day. According to them, the main reason was the ambition of individuals to be super rich in terms of material wealth. To achieve their goal, people go to any extent and pursue ethical or unethical means to acquire the same. Parents and teachers need to teach kids to be satisfied with their needs. From childhood, children should be able to manage different pressures independently. Children learn from society and adapt to ethical or unethical means to win the game. Achievement is considered more important than behaviour.

In the Gurukul, children knew they were an extension of the Supreme. The pressure of achievement was a combination of the Divine's grace and commitment to the child in an ethical manner. Individuals paid gratitude to the Divine / Guru for achieving success. A seed to blossom requires suitable soil, temperature, water, appropriate climate, healthy grains, and sowing at the right time. In the rainy season, rice will grow; however, wheat will get destroyed. Similarly, for an individual to succeed, it is not only his effort; other known and unknown factors like environmental factors also play an essential role.

After the discourse, I bathed at Sethani Ghat. While at the Ghat, I listened to Sadhus engaged in interesting discussions about the significance of colours and their associations with each day. I learned that Monday is associated with Lord Shiva and Chandra (the Moon God), and the colour of the day is white. Tuesday is associated with Mars, and the designated colour is bright red. Wednesday is linked to Mercury, and green is the chosen colour. Thursday is governed by Jupiter, and the preferred colour is yellow. Friday is connected to Venus, and the colour is light blue, while Saturday is associated with Lord Shani, with black or dark blue as the preferred choice. Sunday is dedicated to Surya (the Sun God), and orange, red, and pink are the related colours.

After listening to the sermon, I picked up my backpack to continue my journey. I proceeded through Hosangabad for five kilometers and then took a village road. Due to the heat, back pain, and boils, I found it challenging to continue walking. I spent the night on the open veranda of Narmada Mandir, Dongarwada. I bathed at the village hand pump in the evening, did aarti and rested. A bhakt came to the Mandir and, after darshan, started discussing parikrama. As he requested, I had dinner in the Mandir fetched by him. The next morning, I resumed walking at 5.30 am, and through a rocky path, reached Randhal, crossed Kewlari River Sangam, and proceeded to Gow Khandeshwar Mahadev Mandir, Kharkheri. The Mandir has a gowshala (cowshed) with over five hundred old cows. In the gowshala, cows are being cared for excellently. After the bath and darshan of Mahadev, I had lunch and an afternoon nap in the Ashram.

On the way to Anwali, I went to a Doctor, examined myself, and took Restalin 500 antibiotics capsules and B-complex tablets. In Gajanan Ashram, Swami Ji, sitting with bakths (devotees) in an open compound, enquired about the cause of my limping. I showed him my back and boils. He told me to rest and insisted that I should get myself examined by a proper Doctor. I informed Swami Ji that I had already seen a doctor and had the required medicines. At around 9.00 pm, he sent a car to Dr Joshi's residence, around fourteen kilometres away. After examination, Dr Joshi gave me four injections of antibiotics, allergy, B- complex, and vitamins. He suggested that I finish my parikrama at the earliest since after 25th May weather will be extremely warm with hot winds, and I will not be able to sustain that. Dr Joshi gave an injection to three other bhakts having joint pains. We all had dinner in the compound, and after that, a bhakt went to drop Dr Joshi in a car. After the Doctor left, I gave pressure points to several bhakts for various ailments at night; they experienced immediate relief. I went to sleep around 1.00 am. Swami Ji and other bhakts left for Mahakaleshwar in three cars around 4.00 am.

After a bath, puja and aarti, I packed my bags and did Narmade Har to others at the Ashram. Pujari Ji requested an elder person to give me fresh milk. In a loud and rough tone, the person told Pujari Ji that he had other errands to complete, and hence, he would not give me fresh milk, and both started arguing. I quietly moved out and proceeded for Babri through Guwari, Ghoghara, and Pathora. Two kilometres before, Babri, a farmer working in his field, stopped me. After exchanging Narmade Har, he asked me a common question: "Where are you from." He offered me water and, after that, fresh kakri (long melon) to eat. Considering the hot weather, he requested me to rest under the mango tree on his farm, mushrooming with moong dal (yellow lentil) crop. After having roti and keri ki sabzi (mango curry) for lunch, I slept under the mango tree for around three hours. Around 4.15 pm, I started walking, and through Babri, Chand Gardh came to Narmada Satsang Ashram, Bhiladiya. I spent the night at the Ashram.

From Bhiladiya through Hamidpur, Goda Gaon, I came to Hanuman Mandir, Birja Kheri. After lunch and rest at the Mandir, I started my journey and, by evening, reached Harihareshwar Mahadev Mandir, Jaloda. The following day, through Goyad Ghat, Bhamouri, I reached Vasundhara Seva Ashram, Handia, around 12.30 pm. At the Ashram, I had lunch with the caretaker. Due to Omkareshwar Dam, parikramawasis have to walk along the road after Handia, and it is possible to have a darshan of Narmada Mai only in Omkareshwar. Therefore, I decided to bathe in Narmada Mai before proceeding to Ratatalia.

From Handia to Ratatalia, the valley between the hills had beautiful landscapes covered with green farms. The sunset had a beautiful glaze of colours and was worth watching. In Ratatalia, I stayed in Mr Dhumalchand Kushwaha's courtyard. Mr Kushwaha works as a night watchman in the field; he is religious and has a big heart. By 7.00 pm, he and his family had dinner. I had reached around 8.00 pm, and the family had to prepare dinner again for me. The dinner was excellent. After a bath and aarti, I had dinner and slept in the open courtyard. Walking on this route was a spiritual experience.

After Ratatalia, I walked on a tar road for four kilometres, surrounded by fields and thereafter three kilometres through dense jungles. I crossed River Anjal and reached Boodhia along the dirt road. I had balbhog at Mr

Jagdish's house, curd at Mohal Lal's house, and through the village road came to Panch Talai. Mr Subash Chandra met me on his farm and requested me to have lunch at his residence. I had lunch at his house and slept in the garage till 4.00 pm. I walked through the village Babar, Sartiya, Nagawa, and Panpar, crossed the river Machak and came to Chawkari around 7.00 pm. I stayed in the palatial house of Mr Santosh, Sarpanch of Chawkari. After completing my evening rituals, we had a long chat. Dinner served at around 10.00 pm was royal. The next morning after getting ready, I did morning puja and aarti. In the morning, I was ready and was about to proceed. Mr Santosh and his wife insisted I have balbhog as the journey would be long and tedious. Early in the morning, she prepared and served hot puri and halwa.

From Chawkari, the area was very picturesque, with domes, valleys, and farms of green moong dal, vegetables and local fruits. Plenty of peacocks were dancing to the tune of nature, and birds chirping was a treat to the ears. Everything was in an appropriate place for the right reason. Happiness prevailed, and I started admiring nature and myself. Every moment was a new experience bringing opportunities, surprises, and joy. I walked through the village roads, surrounded by farms, up to Pokharni and along the State Highway to Mata Mandir, Dagarkheri. After lunch and rest, I walked around fifteen kilometres and reached Someshwar Mahadev Mandir, Rampuri, late at night. The area between Pokharni to Rampuri has hills, a semi-forest, trim bushes, rocky soils, and a few farms. I spent the night in the Mandir.

Rampuri onwards, I took SH-15 and came to Chanera (Naya Harshud). The area along the highway after Rampuri was very fertile. At Chanera, I had balbhog (breakfast) at a stall and, through a connecting path, came to Selda Maal via Charu Khera. At Selda Maal, I had lunch at Shri Ram Karan's house. He lives in a cluster with tiny mud houses built for poor people as punarwas (alternate housing built after the village got submerged in Narmada Dam). After lunch and rest, I walked through a few kilometres of jungle road to Hanuman Mandir, Sulja. Other Parikramawasis were already staying in the Mandir. All of us went to Mr Tomar's house for dinner. Excellent preparation of dal and vegetables with hot roti made us overeat. His daughter was suffering from acute back pain and stomach disorder. I gave her pressure points, and relief was immediate. As we were away for dinner in the evening, a monkey took my ghee container away. Without twig and ghee, I performed aarti with an agarbatti (scene stick). In the morning, Mr Omar found the container behind the Temple, came in a car for four kilometres, and handed the same to me.

I walked through the village road and reached Durga Mandir, Mundi. The Temple is in the heart of the Mundi town. After balbhog at Durga Mandir, I came along the highway to Mata Mandir, Bhamori, by afternoon. The outside temperature in the afternoon was around forty degrees Celsius. It was challenging to walk barefoot in the courtyard of the Temple. I had to fetch water, and the sole of my feet boiled while I walked to the hand pump. Pandit Anupam Shastri built the Temple from the donations he received. I had bhog prasad of Mata Ji for lunch.

From Bhamori, I missed a road and had to walk for a few extra kilometres. In the afternoon, I walked fifteen kilometres to reach Mekalsuta Dham, Aatuutkhas. The Ashram is on the main road. Maharaj Ji (Saint) was about to close the gate when I arrived around 9.30 pm. All of the bakths had dinner and slept. Maharaj woke them to prepare dinner for me. They prepared bajra (pearl millet flour) ki roti with a spoonful of ghee, a vegetarian curry and served me at 11.00 pm.

On 25th May 2019, I started early from Aatuutkhas and walked twelve kilometres to reach Hatibaba Ashram. After darshan of the Lord at the Ashram, I proceeded to Chitabur through the canal dust road. The Canal Road had lots of loose stones and pebbles, which acted as acupressure points for the sole. The Outside weather was scorching, and walking proved to be a challenge. By noon I reached Narmada Mandir, Chitabur. A lady sitting on the veranda of her house across the Mandir called me for lunch. She served local cuisine, which I enjoyed. After lunch and a nap in the Mandir, I started for Omkareshwar in the afternoon. From Chitabur to Anjrudh, I walked on the tar road for two kilometres and then crossed the jungle. The jungle path had loose and slippery stones/pebbles. Ascent and descent were steep, with no one to guide or any direction signs. I missed the road and went in another direction; however, one passerby redirected me to the right path. After crossing the hills at Dhakia, I came to Omkareshwar. While travelling through the hilltop, I experienced a change within.

Since I was exhausted, I rested and drank two litres of water at the foothills. On the outskirts of Omkareshwar, I met a bhakt whose wife suffered from thyroid problems. On giving acupressure points to her, the pain subsided, and she went to sleep. After that, I continued my last lap of the journey to Gajanan Ashram, Omkareshwar.

During Narmada Parikrama, I enjoyed cross-country walks through the jungles, hills, sand, farms, tar road, parikrama marg, village roads, and pagdandi. I enjoyed moment by moment and ensured to censor myself from past experiences or anticipation of the future. In the Narmada Valley, one can see "Nishkan Karma' (selfless or desireless action) among sevaks, not knowing them, serving parikramawasis with dedication and devotion. After parikramawasis leave, the relationship collapses without contact or expectations. My experience also taught me to be happy even if basic needs are unfulfilled. It was a play of the Divine to save me from disappointments or harassment and prepare me for more inconceivable bliss.

The conditions during the parikrama kept on changing. At times it was supportive, sometimes stressful or apprehensive. I started my Narmada Parikrama in winter, having near-zero Centigrade temperatures. Moving ahead in April and May, I walked in forty-plus-degree centigrade temperatures at noon. In Shoolpaneshwar ki Jhari and jungle areas, I walked in rugged terrain and conditions, mostly all alone. In plains, the journey was easy. Divine blessing and a higher purpose helped me embark on my parikrama journey during different weather conditions and terrain. Under all circumstances, l experienced fullness and bliss. This experience gave me the extra muscle to keep moving ahead and carefully perform duties irrespective of the surroundings.

My parents, Mrs Vijay Lakshmi Mishra and Mr Indranath Mishra reached Omkareshwar on 23rd May 2019 and stayed in Gajanan Ashram. The next day my wife, Mrs Neeru Mishra and daughter Meenakshi Mishra also checked in at Gajanan Ashram. The Ashram is well managed, provides free accommodation and food for parikramawasis, and has nominal charges for others. With the help of Acharya Anil Das, my wife finalised the entire program of the Udaypan (closing ceremony of a spiritual performance), including location, cooks, and the menu for kanya bhojan, bhandara, gifts, and dakshina. They decided to call around one hundred eight girls for kanya bhojan and approximately fifty-one Brahmins for bhandara. Acharya Anil Das took responsible for sending invitation to girl children and Brahmins. By evening Acharya and my wife did essential purchases and completed all the arrangements.

On 26th May 2019, I did the Udaypan of Narmada Parikrama at Gomukh Ghat under the guidance of Acharya Anil Das. After the ceremony, we performed kanya bhojan for young girls (children) and bhandara for revered learned Brahmins.

The entire journey enhanced my inner wisdom, spirituality, and bliss. It helped me witness rediscover my unique Self and the ability to recognise the expansive cultural contribution of our ancient wisdom, indigenous rituals, and ceremonies.

In the lap of nature, I relished my new way of life, a state of deep awareness, connectedness, and peace. An excellent belief in dynamism, tranquillity, and connection with superior forces became intense through the passage. My body and mind adjusted, aligned, absorbed, and immersed in parikrama. With one-point awareness and full attention, everything worked together in complete harmony. A peak performance, an optimum level of clarity and direction, adjustment, intense deliberation on the "now", moving ahead without a detailed plan for every step, not thinking about every accomplishment but just letting it unfold, became a new way of life for me. My sense of ego, opinion, uncertainties, and reminiscences melted. I was unaware of my inhibition, hunger, thirst, fatigue, or surroundings. Actions became effortless and fluid, with the heightened awareness of the here and now. Time seemed to slow down, and I started experiencing the delight of Divine ecstasy.

Throughout Narmada Valley, powerful magnetic waves were in abundance. All my body energy centres got energised in her lap, and the world within the two ears united. During parikrama, the focus was on now, the mind got directed within, and dhyana (meditation) happened effortlessly. I witnessed layers of my ego, impurities and imperfections melting. I felt united with the Divine and her creation. I was fortunate to spend time in spiritual discourses, bhajan, wisdom and insight, equality, compassionate culture, good thoughts, sacrament and discipline. I realised that none could harm us if we genuinely and unconditionally surrender ourselves to the Divine. Narmada Mai blissfully unfolded the path to attain self-realisation, and with her blessings, I have gained the muscle to walk on the Divine path.

OM Peace, Peace, Peace

Narmade Har.

Reality

"Karmanye vaadhikaaraste maa phaleshu kadaachana;
Maa karmaphalaheturbhoor maa tesango'stwakarmani"

"Having taught Arjuna the eternal nature of the Atman, Lord Krishna turns to the performance of action without expectation of the fruit. A man should not concern himself about the fruit of the action, like gain and loss, victory and defeat. These are in the hands of the Lord. He should perform all actions with a balanced mind, calmly enduring the pairs of opposites like heat and cold, pleasure and pain that inevitably manifest during an action. Krishna advises Arjuna to fight, free from desire for acquisition of kingdom or preservation of it".

- Swami Sivananda

Revolution in scientific advancement during the last century has ensured economic development, improved lifestyle and comfort. Despite progress, the happiness quotient is decreasing. As per the World Bank top ten countries in 2020 by nominal GDP in receding order are the United States, China, Japan, Germany, India, United Kingdom, France, Italy, Brazil and Canada, respectively. Surprisingly, despite the rising living standards, the happiness quotient is declining due to a sense of emptiness with growing human desires. Top countries by GDP do not find a similar place in the UN World Happiness Report 2020 ranking. The United States of America ranks at number 18, China at 94, Japan at 62, Germany at 17, India at 144, the United Kingdom at 13, France at 23, Italy at 30, Brazil at 32 and Canada at 14, respectively.

UN Sustainability Report states that more than seven hundred million people still live in extreme poverty, one-third of the world's food gets wasted, yet 821 million people are undernourished, water scarcity affects more than 40% of the world's population, 9 out of 10 urban residents breathe polluted air and by 2050 the equivalent of the three planets will be required to sustain current lifestyle. Global emission of carbon dioxide (CO_2) has increased by 50% since 1990; in the last three centuries, the world has lost 35 per cent of forests; and in 2018, the number of people fleeing war, persecution and conflict exceeded seventy million. What an illusion! –in pursuit of happiness, individuals and society spend their prime time and energy chasing worldly wealth. The fact is that financially rich nations or people are not the happiest lot.

Unhappiness, conflict, physical and mental diseases, hatred and discord, are witnessed globally from the macro to the micro levels. Of many core aspects of human life, profession, wealth creation, and validation have become the yardstick for success. Most people waste their prime energy on illusionary happiness while satisfying their lust and mundane desires and accumulating trivial worldly wealth or fame.

With all the Divinity of Narmada Mai, sand within her remains sand and does not transform into water. Similarly, an individual living under the control of their senses with lust, anger, greed, attachment, ego, hatred, and jealousy remains lifeless due to inappropriate memories of the past or future unethical expectations.

Every individual is under the dominance of one of the three flavours, Swatta (moral, virtue and goodness), Rajas (passion and moral blindness) and Tamas (ignorance and darkness), and accordingly, they experience the world. Human birth is a precious gift of God. We are blessed with human life to utilise resources and transform ourselves to the highest level of self-realisation, attain oneness with the Divine and be free from the cycle of birth and death.

The human body is composed of five elements called panch bhoota - agni (fire), vayu (wind), dharti (earth), jal (water) and aakash (space). The earth element is most condensed, followed by water, fire, air and ether. Divine creation is separated predominantly by ether element, and an invisible force within it connects the entire universe. The subtle energy within the space of nature, plants, animals, and humans is responsible for maintenance and destruction.

Our body is a Temple, and the Atma is pure consciousness. The Temple needs to be in an excellent condition to realise self-awareness. An individual is a part of his intellect, mind, emotions and organs. Our sense organs, mind, intellect, memory, and ego affect how we think, speak and act. An individual perceives and ties himself to signals received through the sense organs, past experiences (vasana), or future expectations. Mind interplays with the memory, tendencies, ego, and refinement of intelligence and then takes action. Usually, the mind reacts based on external stimuli and past experiences. As a person matures, the discriminating power of intellect guides his mind. When an individual surrenders to the Divine, he is fully protected, attains self-consciousness, and is not affected by his karma

– good or bad. A person not guided by HIM (Divine) must suffer the consequences of his action – good or bad.

Happiness flows out of a healthy system; fulfilment, love, peace, and harmony come with it. Unfortunately, unregulated life causes an imbalance in the nervous system. It results in weight gain, agitation, unregulated blood pressure, diabetes, dullness, and other illnesses. As an individual gets exhausted, exhalation seems heavier. An individual easily gets agitated with unfulfilled worldly desires, negative thoughts or feelings. During agitation, prana (breath) becomes unsteady with shorter inhalation. Breath quivers when an individual is under fear or anxiety.

To be healthy, an individual needs to be compassionate to the self and maintain a healthy spiritual, mental and physical body. The happening of the world, relationships within the universe, place, and situations of life is a theatre play. The outer world is a reflection, whereas the inner self is the stage. To maintain good health, individuals must be conscious of their thoughts, beliefs, and actions that help them remain positive even in adverse circumstances. People with strong will can overcome their emotional and physical discomfort or disability and evolve. People with chronic disability have also evolved, and history is a witness.

The human brain is the unit microcosm plus the collection of cells within the body, having intimate associations and relationships. Cells have a short life and require air (oxygen), water, light, heat and food to grow. Food consumed by an individual affects the cells and consequently affects the individual. It is beneficial to have sattvic (light and healthy) food daily. Avoid consuming rajasic (mutative) food as far as feasible, and do not consume tamasic (static) food.

Preparation, serving, and eating of food need to take place in a positive environment as it affects the vitality of the food. Offer the food to the Divine with devotion, show gratitude, and after that, consume the food. While offering the food to the Divine with mantras, purification happens; the energy level enhances, giving optimum energy and matter to the consumer. The temperament of a person consuming the food affects the absorption and digestion of food. Food changes its forms, and a chemical reaction occurs during its movement in the digestive system, from the mouth to the throat, large intestine, and small intestine. Finally, the residue leaves the body through the anus differently.

The mental spectrum has an ego on one side and ignorance on the other. Optimum performance comes when one takes the middle path. With ego, individuals do not see the need for learning and growth; with ignorance, one is unaware of the way. Modifications of the inner self due to illusion, wrong belief and ego cloud the mind and are responsible for all sufferings (kleshas). A balanced approach to life comes through self-significance rather than sense-indulgence. An individual needs to have a higher purpose, moderate time for appropriate fitness and balance the self in the spiritual, mental, emotional and physical arena to move ahead in the path of self-realisation.

On the spiritual path, consciousness guides and balances the self with appropriate checks and balances. The saying, 'where attention goes, energy flows,' is a fundamental truth. Taking ethical and concentrated action is essential for building a relationship with the goal. With a feeling of oneness, an individual can accept everything reasonably with clarity and purity. In turn, it kindles a higher form of energy within us – love, compassion, enthusiasm, devotion and commitment. Remain humble in case of achievement and resilient if the result is not as expected or in our favour. In the absence of regrets, fear, or anxiety - the mind turns within, the individual gains strength and becomes peaceful, knowledge widens, calmness prevails, and the capability to climb the peak builds up.

Humans can live a balanced life, reach lasting happiness, and attain inner calm through a natural sense of wholeness and well-being. By continuously being aware of their beliefs, thoughts, feelings, actions, and energy, one can shred negativity, reinforce positive experiences, imprint happiness, and be on the right path. The key is to remain focused on their higher purpose in life and control their prana, thoughts, words, food, association, habits, and deeds. It helps to communicate within self and with the Divine and a Guru. By doing so, an individual moves ahead in the spiritual path, get rids of all distractions and samskaras and starts enjoying happiness and bliss.

Memory recreates what is already in the mind. Perception and vibration are embedded in the nerve cells within and differ according to the vibration they carry. Over time perception and vibrations stored in the nerve cells moves to the subconscious mind (citta) or ectoplasm mind and get permanently grounded. Our energy gets propelled out of our mind as thoughts, feelings, and actions. It loses intensity over time if we tend to focus outside ourselves. A self-absorbed and peaceful person does not worry or overthink; he is full of positivity and enthusiasm. Knowing ourselves is the purpose of life and the source of lasting bliss. Happiness comes from loving the self and others and seeing oneness in all. Having attained self-knowledge, the individual remains calm in achievements and sufferings, emerges from miseries, and uplifts the self to ecstasy.

In the words of Swami Sivananda, "Work cannot bring misery. It is attachment and identification to work that brings in all sorts of worries, troubles and unhappiness. Understand the secret of Karma Yoga and work without attachment and identification. You will soon attain God-consciousness."

Happiness or unhappiness is an outcome of the expected results. Our expectations and actions come from our samskara, memory, ego, intelligence, experience and expectations. We perceive and experience the outer world through our senses, which may or may not be reality. Happiness flows from within rather than external sources. A resilient individual sees an opportunity in an adverse situation, whereas an ordinary person sees a disaster and curses himself.

Due to their highly complex mixture of will, intellect and feelings, human beings have the power to manifest, uplift, and transform themselves based on their intention, emotion, enthusiasm, self-determination, reasoning, pre-action, action, and post-action contemplation. Human beings have a highly evolved sophisticated processor and unlimited mental storage capacity. They have the intellectual capabilities to solve highly complex situations. The power to discriminate, make choices, take action, control and change the environment, and transform themselves into a higher state of being is unique to humans.

Human existence is through four states of awareness: jagrat (awake), swapna (dream), sushupti (deep sleep), and turiya (super consciousness). In a waking state, an individual is aware of the daily world. The dream state (subtle body) is inward-knowing, subtle and burning. In a deep sleep state (causal body), the underlying ground of consciousness is undistracted; it moves to a subjective world. In turiya, both absolute and relative are transcended. It is the true state of experience of the infinite and non-different, free from the dualistic experience which results from the attempts to conceptualise.

Spiritual practice brings positive thoughts, refreshes, regenerates, and tranquilises the body, mind, intelligence, memory, ego, lust, jealousy and anger. It melts blockages from the skin to bone and head to toe, leading to proper respiration, blood circulation, and digestion. When chitta (subconscious mind) is without vrittis (innermost thoughts) for an extended period, the energy of samskaras - lust, anger, greed, ego, hatred and jealousy gets erased. Right knowledge prevails; discrimination between right and wrong deepens. It leads to Purusharth (act by the will of super consciousness). It helps the individual transcendent in Universal Consciousness (Samadhi), the arena of ultimate bliss.

Great Saints, Rishis, and Philosophers of India have dwelt upon the subject of human proficiency and efficiency at length. A detailed description in Sanatana Dharma scriptures shows the way concerning composite human development. Scriptures have laid down a clear path for self-realisation. Shravan (hearing the truth), manan (contemplating the truth) and nididhyasan (living and breathing the truth) are pillars of spiritual upliftment. Nididhyasan is internalising of Shravan and Manan. The ratio between Shravan to Manan is roughly 1:99. Nididhyasan is sahaja (spontaneous and natural) when an individual unbiasedly listens to the truth from authentic sources, contemplates and takes action accordingly over time.

Scriptures have laid down systematic studies for removing three defects of the mind - mala or impurity, vikshepa or tossing, avarana or veil. The practice of Karma Yoga, Bhakti Yoga, Raja Yoga and Jnana Yoga, are four spiritual paths laid down for the seekers depending upon an individual's temperament, leading to their communion with the Divine. In Karma Yoga the active aspect of mind is involved; in Bhakti Yoga, the emotional aspect; in Raja Yoga, the mystical aspect; in Jnana Yoga, the intellectual aspect. Knowledge of the true self and all –round perfection in life, is facilitated by the Divine as a seeker commit themself to love, sewa (selfless service), sadhana (worship), meditation and realisation.

Sage Patanjali, in Yoga Sutras, states, "yogas chitta vritti nirodhah." Yoga restrains the fluctuation of Chitta (mind stuff) through control of vrittis (mental affliction). Memories, thoughts and tendencies get erased if an individual dwells in the union of the inner self. Manas (mind), buddhi (determinative faculty/ intelligence), chitta (memory), and ahankar (ego) are karana (internal instruments). The mind takes impressions from the sense organs, checks with chitta–ahankar–vrittis, and presents it to the intellect. The discriminatory faculty takes a decision and conveys it to the mind. Through the five senses, the mind experiences the outer world.

He (the Sage) has laid down intricacies of yoga (a process of human purification) to liberate an individual from kleshas (afflictions) and action-reaction interlace and attain oneness with the Divine. His work of inner experience gives a glimpse of introspective contemplation-yama (abstinences), niyama (observances), asana (yoga), pranayama (breath control), pratyahara (withdrawal of the senses), dharana (concentration of the mind), dhyana (meditation), and samadhi (liberation).

Yama (social discipline) and niyama (self-restraint) act as a glue to balance the need of the self and society. Individuals must follow universal ethical guidelines, restraints, and observances to control evil and negative thoughts. Faith, gratitude and forgiveness help to build trust, love, compassion, peace, and harmony within self and society.

A healthy body has a healthy mind. Yoga is the most advanced scientific method to maintain a healthy mind-body. The connection and interrelation of consciousness and body with prana become natural during asana and pranayama. Prana is the subtle force that provides life, the connecting link between matter and energy, mind and consciousness, and is necessary for functioning all parts - physical and superphysical. With inhalation, energy enhances, and during exhalation of breath, calmness prevails, and breath slows down. Energy blocked in the nerves and chakras gets released, and prana aligns the body with the Atma and the Divine.

In pratyahara, one isolates self from the world's distractions by controlling the senses. Sadhana helps an individual control his thoughts and feelings, experience stability, and attain inner peace. Dharana helps an individual focus and absorb for an extended period on the object of concentration.

A sadhak (Divine seeker) can attain siddhis or psychic accomplishments through the practice of dharana (concentration of the mind) and dhyana (meditation) on various aspects of the universe, also the final stage is set for the realisation of the highest state of samadhi (liberation). Siddhis attained during the process may divert the mind towards the fruit of siddhis and lead to downfall. Devotees who want to achieve self-realisation must continue their practice of samadhi rather than get involved in siddhis. Siddhis should not be used to demonstrate one's extraordinary powers as it boosts the ego and causes spiritual downfall. After samadhi and kaivalya, all the gunas – sattvic, rajasic, and tamasic, stand dissolved. After that, the sadhak (Divine seeker) enjoys absolute bliss beyond ordinary beings' comprehension. Bliss is everlasting and ever-increasing, as against an individual's normal enjoyment in life. Worldly happiness is only momentarily.

Lord Krishna in Bhagavad Gita reveals the Sanatan dharma (spiritual path to achieve perfection of self), pure knowledge, eternal truth, the significance of yoga, selfless action, varn (classification of four levels of meditation and worship), yagna (worship and meditation). Gita has laid down steps to destroy our inner devilish flavour and invoke Divinity within through yagna and karma (devotional action). Under the guidance of an enlightened Saint / Guru, an individual moves up the ladder of spiritual evolution and ultimately has the auspicious sight of the Divine and merges with the Supreme Consciousness. Lord Krishna has emphasised that He will give all his devotees Jnana (knowledge of pure consciousness).

Bhakti Yoga lays a simple path of pure devotion to attain the truth (pure knowledge), bliss, and liberation from the cycles of birth and death. The process is to surrender the self to the Divine by offering prayer, worship, singing devotional songs in praise of the Lord (bhajans), japa (mantra chanting), lila (hearing the Divine's play), svadhyaya (studying of scriptures), sewa (selfless service), serving the Divine and His lotus feet with full dedication. When engrained in mind, Japa (bija mantra chanting) sustains our life, makes the mind pleasant, and uplifts spirituality. When repeated regularly, Japa wades off unnecessary negative thoughts and raises consciousness. Mantra chanting has a cleansing effect on the body, mind, and emotions. Through yoga, negative memories get erased, resulting in harmful tendencies and habits getting dissolved.

Narmada Parikrama is a comprehensive and integrated path of Raja Yoga (scientific step-by-step approach of mind control), Jnana Yoga (path of wisdom), Karma Yoga (selfless action) and Bhakti Yoga (exclusive devotion to the Lord) for self-realisation – to awaken awareness of the Divinity within. Parikramawasis must equip themselves and be ready to fight the inner war between the devilish and the Divine, by committing to right inquiry (vicara), constant self-analysis (viveka), sadhana, sewa, bhakti, yoga and meditation.

During the Anusthan ceremony at Omkareshwar, I pledged to lead a simple life and control my negative behaviour of hoarding, untruthfulness, laziness, selfishness, or the like through restraints or observances. Throughout Narmada Parikrama, I did commit to the sankalpa, practised sadhana, japa and meditation, selfless sewa, and teachings of the Saints. My thoughts and actions helped me clear undesired memories and related worldly lust and anger. Over time, my prana aligned, positive thoughts flew in a continuum, and I felt spellbound in Divine bliss.

My experience during parikrama from beginning to end was packed with extraordinary physical, mental and spiritual experiences. As the complexity increased, endurance to complete the parikrama grew within. A few marvels - on day one, I sprained my knees. A Saint and Mataji at Bari Ali helped me overcome body and mind disturbances. A Saint seeing me wearing a knee cap applied medicinal oil, and within minutes the pain vanished. Unable to cross the river, parikramawasis suddenly appeared and, leaving their belongings, helped me cross the stream. Skin disease for the last three decades got cured during the parikrama. I got rid of constipation, lack of saliva in the mouth, and weakness became history. From childhood, I was used to drinking filtered water, eating timely food without spices and chillies, sleeping at a pleasant and comfortable temperature, and so on. I started drinking water from a hand pump and Narmada Mai. I also walked in the scorching heat without having wholesome food or drinking water, slept in the cold weather under the open sky or by the side of the road or alone in an isolated place.

When I lost my way in the jungle, people appeared, showed me the right track, and suddenly disappeared. Parikramawasis joined when the terrain was challenging. After escorting me to the appropriate place, I was left alone for meditation and self-reflection. Unknown dogs escorted me to the right path. I witnessed the generous donations the bakths gave without any discrimination or strings attached. Bhakts who took care of parikramawasi were a happier lot. Scripture narrates that subtle energy in the form of blessing moves the donor from a scarcity mindset to abundance – an essential aspect of self-evolution.

I spent many days walking through remote locations, including the jungles. Rugged terrain played an excellent role as it kept me focused and safe. Engagement with the self, helped me isolate myself from external distractions. Regular tests of health and fitness acted as a safety valve. Due to my samskaras, I suffered from illness. However, by the grace of Narmada Mai, sickness happened only in places having well-established medical facilities. Hospitals and Doctors gave free treatment, and parikramawasis delayed their journey to escort me to the hospital and took care until I recovered. Obstacles and hindrances strengthened my performance and spiritual growth positively. I was pleased to help those who needed my guidance regarding their carrier. To extend possible, I also helped people.

I came across Gurus in the form of Saints, pundits, bhakts, devotees, people and sentient beings. Unfolding the path of awakening knowledge during the parikrama was enlightening. It started with simple discourses and experiences. Then, the complexities of spirituality and extraordinary experiences kept enhancing, and doubts got cleared at an appropriate time. The awareness that I am the Atma (consciousness), hidden by layers of my samskaras, like the Sun hidden by clouds, cannot be seen, opened the door of wisdom. The Divine is the creator of energy in each karn (atom); the truth is pure beyond space and time, all-pervading, all-powerful and all-knowing, and beyond comprehension became apparent.

Opportunities to listen to scriptures - Ramayana, Shrimad Bhagawat, Bhagavad Gita, Shiva Parana, and Durga Saptashi were a blessing and renewal of true knowledge. By singing devotional songs and performing selfless sewa, I developed a deep bond with devotion, and it helped me to subdue my ego. Awareness enhanced that all beings – earth, water, air, environment, plant, bird, animal and human beings are creations of the Divine.

During parikrama, I did witness my negative memories, propensities, ego, impurities, and flaws getting dissolved. I always felt united with the Divine and her creation. My realisation that no one can harm me if I surrender to the Divine is the most incredible wisdom. I learnt from Sages and enlightened individuals how to communicate respectfully and with dignity and be careful and modest with words. My lessons in communication did help me rise above small, lifeless, and useless talk. With love and devotion, sadachar (ethical and virtuous behaviour) and sadhana (disciplined and dedicated spiritual practice), my energy remained vibrant and alive, and love spread within and outside. A big realisation - it is fruitless to only concentrate on external desires, validation, and excessive attachment to people, things or positions. Once the soul leaves the body, everything generated, created or accumulated at a physical level is left behind. The consciousness moves on to its journey.

In the spiritual laboratory of the parikrama, I was fortunate to have the opportunity to unveil proper knowledge about myself. The parikrama was the training ground to walk the path towards self-transformation and realisation. Many puzzles of life got resolved. I enjoyed the bliss of nature, consciousness and calmness within. Harmful tendencies and destructive internal dialogues got reduced, and I invoked the flavour of love, compassion and enthusiasm on demand. I did climb the first few steps on the ladder of spiritual growth, and I know the path to move forward. However, I need to commit myself to walking the path. I have tried to explain what words can describe. Many extraordinary experiences (anubhava) are beyond words. Therefore, I have highlighted a few of them for the welfare of humanity.

I am grateful to you for reading about the extraordinary experiences of Narmada Parikrama. Enjoy the ecstasy of your true self by cementing yourself through breathing and living the Divine Truth. I conclude by quoting a shloka from chapter twelve of Srimad Bhagavad Gita.

मय्येवमनआधत्स्वमयिबुद्धिंनिवेशय।
निवसिष्यसिमय्येवअतऊर्ध्वंनसंशयः ॥ ८॥

**mayyēva mana ādhatsva
mayi buddhiṁ nivēśaya /**

**nivasiṣyasi mayyēva ata
ūrdhvaṁ na saṁśayaḥ // 8 //**

Fix your mind and intellect only on ME (Divine); and thereafter you will dwell in ME. Don't have an iota of doubt about this.

OM Peace, Peace, Peace

Narmade Har.

Black Eagle Books

www.blackeaglebooks.org
info@blackeaglebooks.org

Black Eagle Books, an independent publisher, was founded as a nonprofit organization in April, 2019. It is our mission to connect and engage the Indian diaspora and the world at large with the best of works of world literature published on a collaborative platform, with special emphasis on foregrounding Contemporary Classics and New Writing.

www.ingramcontent.com/pod-product-compliance
Lightning Source LLC
Chambersburg PA
CBHW030227100526
44585CB00012BA/313